SMITTEN WITH SQUASH

MINNESOTA
HISTORICAL
SOCIETY PRESS

SMITTEN WITH SQUASH

AMANDA KAY PAA

the *Northern* plate

the orthern plate

Smitten with Squash is the fourth book in the Northern Plate series, celebrating the bounty of the Upper Midwest by focusing on a single ingredient, exploring its historical uses as well as culinary applications across a range of dishes. *Rhubarb Renaissance* by Kim Ode, *Modern Maple* by Teresa Marrone, and *Sweet Corn Spectacular* by Marie Porter are other books in the series.

www.mhspress.org

The Minnesota Historical Society Press is a member of the Association of American University Presses.

Manufactured in the United States of America

10 9 8 7 6 5 4 3 2

♾ The paper used in this publication meets the minimum requirements of the American National Standard for Information Sciences—Permanence for Printed Library Materials, ANSI Z39.48–1984.

International Standard Book Number
ISBN: 978-0-87351-939-7 (paper)

LIBRARY OF CONGRESS CATALOGING-IN-PUBLICATION DATA
Paa, Amanda, 1984–
Smitten with squash / Amanda Paa.
    pages cm
Summary: "Expand your squash repertoire with more than 70 creative recipes. This abundant vegetable spans the seasons, offering a delicious base on which to build inspired multicultural dishes, bringing forth assertive flavors from savory to sweet"— Provided by publisher.
Includes bibliographical references and index.
ISBN 978-0-87351-939-7 (paperback)
1. Cooking (Squash) 2. Squashes. I. Title.

TX803.S67P33 2014
641.6'562—dc23

2014013244

....

Smitten with Squash was designed and set in type by Cathy Spengler.
The typefaces are Chaparral, TheSans, and Aviano.

Finished dishes photographed by Amanda Kay Paa.

Special love and appreciation to

> *my companion and best friend Brian, who supported me through every part of this journey, eating more squash than he ever probably wished to and allowing me to immerse myself in what I love;*

> *my closest friends, who have cheered me on, testing recipes and giving me honest opinions, and who inspire me with their own brilliance in the kitchen;*

> *my mom and dad, for their encouragement to always follow my passion;*

> *Carol, the über-knowledgable "Squash Lady" of the St. Paul Farmers Market, who graciously taught me about many different varieties and supplied me with much of the squash I used for testing;*

> *all the other farmers I conversed with, who educated me on the growing of squash here in the Midwest;*

> *the amazing food community of the Twin Cities area that has given me a voice and supported me in the creation of the book; and*

> *all of you who are reading this. Thank you.*

> ....

CONTENTS

SMITTEN WITH SQUASH

INTRODUCTION:
GROW, EAT,
AND LOVE

On a chilly October morning, a stroll through my favorite farmers market yielded a large sack of winter squash from a lone man in the last row, his cheeks cherry red from the harsh wind. Unsure what to do with these odd-shaped ugly ducklings, I knew I was yearning for comfort food, seeking solace from a constant internal roar brought on by a chaotic job. Winter squash were not part of my cooking routine, but I sank into a rhythm as I peeled away the sandy brown rind of a butternut squash. As I revealed its gorgeous burnt-orange flesh, appreciation for the beauty of this squash struck me. After a quick online search, I decided to make an intriguing risotto recipe with one of the squash that the lone man's hands had carefully fostered. As I stirred with a patient hand, the golden flecks of squash melting in the heat, my soul was soothed. The aromatic finished dish was perfect and creamy, as lush and colorful as the deepest hues of autumn—exactly what I needed on that blustery day.

From that moment, my passion for squash seemed limitless, and I sought to cook with all varieties, from the slender yellow or green thin-skinned summer squash to the heavy and bulbous winter varieties like red kuri, its rugged orange skin meant for winter preservation. The possibilities are truly endless thanks to squash's versatility. Join me in celebrating the seasons with seventy-five delicious recipes that highlight the joy of squash from sweet to savory, breakfast to dessert, inspired by myriad cultural cuisines. I hope this book brings you together with others in sharing health, happiness, and a magical delight in everything this special vegetable has to offer. Equal parts cookbook, journal, and insider knowledge, *Smitten with Squash* is the result of my ever-growing love for this family of food and the practice of living well.

> *Surely one of the greatest satisfactions of life is to cook a really delicious meal, a meal that nourishes the body and cheers the spirit, and may be remembered with pleasure for a long time to come.*
> **— R. ELLIOT**

Coming from such a large family, squash can be a bit overwhelming, but I'm hoping this book will become your trusted resource for identifying and cooking with summer and winter squash. I'm excited to have you dive deeper into common varieties like zucchini, butternut, and acorn, but what I'm busting at the seams to share with you is the versatility of other varieties that you've probably seen and passed by at your local market, unsure of what to do with them. I'm truly smitten with this family and can't wait for you to explore the world of flavors, cooking techniques, and pure deliciousness that I've discovered. So are you ready? It's time to meet the golden children of the Cucurbit family, summer and winter squash.

Although the botanical names of plant families can be difficult to keep track of as well as pronounce, understanding their backgrounds can be helpful in learning how to identify them. The Cucurbit family, commonly referred to as the gourd family, includes cucumbers, melons, chayotes, and pumpkins as well as over a hundred varieties of squash in three different families: Cucurbita maxima, Cucurbita moschata, and Cucurbita pepo. They have beautiful long, flowing vines that trail along the ground, providing protection for the roots of the annual plants. Spiraled tendrils and leaves resembling tiny hearts bring the fruit to life in sunny yellow flowers that hold the power of the mighty and curvaceous squash that will evolve. While we commonly refer to them as vegetables, squash are actually a fruit because they contain seeds.

Squash is considered a monumental vegetable in many historians' eyes, as it is presumed to be the plant that graduated hunters and gatherers to growers. Dustings of twelve-thousand-year-old Cucurbita seeds were found in the caves of Ecuador, and much of its history is rooted in southern Mexico. Domestication of other crops such as corn and beans didn't begin until four thousand years later, which speaks to Cucurbita's importance in the food chain. Over ten thousand years, the plants gradually migrated north with native populations. Cultivation became widespread as people discovered that when squash were grown with corn and beans, all three thrived. Referred to as the "Three Sisters" of Indian agriculture, they became the first form of intercropping. Native Americans discovered that the tall, straight stalks of corn were just right for the climbing vines of the beans, whose roots captured nitrogen from the air, enriching the soil for the corn. The large squash leaves covered the ground, protecting and shading the shallow roots. It may be thousands of years later, but Midwest farmers are still using this same technique to bring us a bountiful harvest—a testament to its brilliance.

Squash, potatoes, parsnips, and onions—vegetables that can last for months during the long and frigid northern winters are a must in every Midwest kitchen. Because eating locally and seasonally is the foundation of my cooking, I would be lost (and really hungry) without an ample supply of squash to take the place of greens, tomatoes, and the likes of warmer months. As I was writing this book and getting to know several growers, I was moved by their dedication and the vulnerability that is part of farming. As *Los Angeles Times* food editor Russ Parsons once said, "Growing food is not the same as manufacturing widgets. It is an endeavor that requires the right circumstances, talent, and more than a little bit of luck. It is an endeavor fraught with the potential for mishap. Bad seed, bad soil, bad weather—all are waiting in line to surprise the unlucky farmer." It's hard for me to imagine a job that risky and difficult. I encourage you to get to know your farmers too and to truly learn about where your food comes from. Trust me: the meals you create from their harvest will taste even better when you know their story.

While squash are not as labor intensive as other vegetables, *strict* daily monitoring during the growing season is required. Pests like the squash vine borer and cucumber beetle can wipe out an entire crop without much warning. Vine borers are orange moths that lay their eggs near the base of squash. The larvae then tunnel inside the stems of both summer and winter squash plants. Gardeners often don't realize anything is wrong until the whole plant starts wilting, and by then it's too late. If this pest does attack, the same type of squash cannot be planted in that soil for three to four years. At that point crop rotation is very important, but because vine borers are strong fliers (sometimes mistaken for wasps) rotation in small gardens has little impact. Squash bugs are also common, though not as devastating. Scouting plants diligently will help gardeners find the bugs before they take over, but it is time consuming. Butternut squash are one of the varieties most resistant to the vine borer, which is why they are so widely available and a good choice to begin growing if you've never planted squash before.

Both summer and winter squash grow best in well-drained, moist soil with long, hot days, a combination sometimes difficult to achieve in the Midwest because of the sporadic weather. If possible, mounding the plants even a few inches will facilitate circulation and encourage proper growth. Once the seedlings have sprouted, cover the area with natural mulch to ward off disease. Additionally, be careful to water only the roots, avoiding the foliage as much as possible to prevent mildew.

HELPFUL HINTS FROM MY KITCHEN TO YOURS

- If possible, buy organically grown squash. Although one would expect the thick skin to protect the flesh from pesticides, the roots of squash are like sponges, soaking up anything that is in the soil. Because of this quality, some farmers will plant squash not as a food crop, but to improve soil quality in between seasons and/or crop rotations. At farmers markets, often the produce is organic but not labeled as such because certification is quite costly, so simply ask vendors about their growing methods before buying.

- Salt is one of the most important ingredients in any recipe, yet it is commonly misused in many kitchens. There's lots of preaching about how oversalting can easily ruin a dish, but that's just as true with undersalting. In my recipes I use kosher salt, as I feel it has the best texture and taste. By tasting as you go instead of once the dish is complete, you'll have a properly seasoned dish. *If you are using table salt, start with a lesser amount than what my recipes call for because it has a much finer grain: 1 teaspoon of table will contain more salt than 1 teaspoon of kosher.*

- One of the best things I ever did to improve my cooking was spending five dollars on an oven thermometer. Even if you buy a brand-new oven, chances are the calibration isn't perfect. After a few issues with baking, I tested my oven and discovered it runs about 35 degrees lower than what it is set at! Still, baking times may differ for many reasons besides temperature, so I've included references as to how things should look or feel when done to help guide you.

- Fresh herbs are a simple way to make any dish taste gourmet without much of a fuss, which is why you'll see them in just about every recipe of mine. Their brightness and balance can bring a meal alive. If in a pinch you have only dried, substitute half the amount of fresh called for because dried are much more concentrated.

- And most of all, I encourage you to make these recipes your own. Missing a few things in the ingredients list? Use what you have on hand, what looks freshest at the market, or what's growing abundantly in your garden. This flexible approach is how my cooking really began to evolve, as sparks of creativity accented each meal I was making. Through many happy accidents I've discovered flavor combinations that would have otherwise been overlooked.

It's safe to say that someone you know, maybe even you, has a gluten intolerance or celiac disease. Three years ago I found out I was one of those people. What at first seemed like something that would be very difficult to manage became one of the best thing that ever happened to my cooking. It opened my eyes to all of the wonderful whole, unprocessed foods that Mother Earth and dedicated farmers provide us with. Real food like farm-raised meat, fresh fruits and eggs, and many whole grains are naturally devoid of gluten but full of pure nourishment. All of the recipes in this cookbook are either naturally gluten free or include adaptations to make them so, as in the case of baked goods.

- All of the recipes in this book have been tested with both regular all-purpose flour and gluten-free all-purpose flour. After extensive experimenting with many gluten-free flour mixes, I recommend Cup4Cup by Williams-Sonoma, which best mimics wheat flour in all characteristics: texture, flavor, and consistency. Although it may be a little more expensive, I have used it with success in everything from fresh pasta to gooey cinnamon rolls. My "gluten-full" guinea pigs can never tell the difference!

  - Measuring gluten-free flour by weight instead of volume is very important because each flour in a mix inevitably weighs a different amount. And since no two mixes are the same, you want to be sure that no matter which mix you are using the amount is equivalent for a recipe. Because people have different techniques for measuring flour, using weight instead of "cups" ensures the amount is identical every time. In most cases, as you'll see in my recipes, 1 cup of all-purpose flour can be substituted with 140 grams of your favorite gluten-free flour blend, except for in certain baked goods where that ratio may differ because of how gluten-free flours absorb liquid.

- Most people who bake with regular flour probably grew up using standard cup measurements, so that is how the recipes read for those using all-purpose flour. If you use cup measurements, don't scoop from the bag with your measuring cup. This technique can compress the flour up to 25 percent, meaning you'll have a lot more flour than what the recipe intended. Instead, use a spoon to fill the measuring cup for the most accurate results.

- Gluten-free flour mix can be expensive, but making your own is always an option, too. I often mix up a big batch of the one listed below to keep on hand to get me through several recipes. I buy the flours from the bulk bins at my co-op, but they are becoming more available in traditional grocery stores and, of course, always online.

GLUTEN-FREE FLOUR MIX

150 grams brown rice flour

225 grams white rice flour

130 grams tapioca starch

155 grams sweet rice flour (also known as glutinous rice flour)

2 teaspoons xanthan gum

Note: Cup4Cup flour and the above Gluten-free Flour Mix both contain xanthan gum, which is needed to make the recipes in this book turn out correctly. If you are using a different gluten-free flour mix, make sure it contains xanthan gum or add it in accordingly.

Summer Squash

Let's face it. Summer squash is promiscuous without even trying to be. The Cucurbita pepo family includes the resilient zucchini, long and slender yellow summer squash, UFO-shaped pattypan, crookneck, eight ball, and many more. And did you know acorn, delicata, and spaghetti squash are in this family as well, even though they're often categorized as winter squash? (Note that their descriptions and recipes appear in the winter squash section because seasonally that's when you'll find them.) Summer squash are ever elusive of danger, outliving all sorts of natural elements—drought or flood, sun or shade, hot days and cool nights. Their tender flesh, smooth edible skin, and mild creaminess have versatility and pure delight in every bite. It's a shame they are sometimes taken for granted, which most often happens when they're growing at the speed of weeds, not vegetables. Although they may not be as beautiful as plump strawberries or juicy heirloom tomatoes, their lengthy "peak" season provides months of sustenance in your kitchen, which is unique in the food world.

Without question these squash provide a plentiful harvest, so a close eye is needed to keep them from getting away from you. Summer squash can grow so quickly that finding ways to eat them (or friends to foist them upon) could become a competitive cooking show. A common scenario: You take a peek in the garden and see several specimens looking trim and tender, but you decide to wait a day to pick them. The next morning you go to gather them, and boom—you've got squash as big as baseball bats staring at you.

The two most common varieties, zucchini and yellow summer squash, can be planted shortly after the last frost in relatively dry soil. They grow best in full sun with fertile and well-drained soil, maturing in about forty to fifty days. Steady moisture is also necessary. As a consumer you'll see them start appearing in midwestern farmers markets in early June, but they are available in grocery stores year round because warmer climates can support their growth. Many wonder what the difference between cooking with all of these tender squash is. In all honesty, I've found that, unlike winter squash, there really isn't much. The one thing I've noticed is that the seeds of yellow squash are larger and more plentiful than those of other varieties.

HARVESTING: Although time consuming, frequent harvesting increases yields, starting with the squash blossoms. Female blossoms will have a soft, fleshy ovary center that develops into the fruit, but the males grow from the branches and only produce pollen. Regular picking—even three to four times a week at midsummer—will ensure the plants produce all season long and will help keep gigantic squash at bay.

IDENTIFICATION:
Harvesting and buying summer squash when they're eight to ten inches in length or smaller is ideal. They should be shiny and feel solid, even giving a little squeak when you run your fingers over their skin. Buying younger, skinnier squash is best because as they grow taller and fatter their skin becomes tougher and the flesh more bland.

Other varieties of summer squash that I have sporadically stumbled upon at midwestern markets include:

- Costata romanesca, an Italian heirloom zucchini with pale, raised ribs that run lengthwise. It definitely has a juicier, sweeter flavor than traditional zucchini, but unless you grow it yourself it is difficult to find at the market because it perishes quickly.

- Eight balls appear in a variety of colors, most often green. They are round and very dense and have a fiberless flesh with hardly any seeds. They slice into perfect rounds and can be baked, steamed, or sautéed like regular zucchini.

- Pattypan are elegant, scalloped yellow and green summer squash. Best when they are small (at the most three inches in diameter), they should have a smooth flesh and can be creamy and buttery in flavor, but don't be surprised to find that some are quite bland. The tinier they are, like the size of a mushroom, the better tasting they'll be.

- Zephyr, a hybrid of the yellow crookneck, is simply beautiful. It's also yellow and slender, but the blossom end looks like it was dip-dyed in light green paint. Not only are zephyrs easy on the eye; they also have a noteworthy nutty taste that other summer squash are devoid of.

STORAGE: Once picked, summer squash are highly perishable. Their freshness deteriorates as soon as they are harvested and start to respire, defined as the rate at which they give off carbon dioxide. Ripening can be slowed by storing them tightly wrapped in dry paper towels within a plastic bag placed in the crisper of the refrigerator for up to four days. Do not wash your squash before storing; moisture accumulation will result in soft, mushy flesh.

THE INSIDE SCOOP: The biggest caveat when cooking with summer squash is their high water content, which can be a positive or negative quality depending on what you are making. For instance, the added water from grated squash in baked goods is extremely beneficial, creating moist and light cakes, breads, and muffins. In other applications like salads or pastas, excess moisture could result in a soggy, diluted dish. To combat this, you will need to salt the squash to draw out the liquid, similar to what you would do with eggplant. Reducing the water content will allow the vegetables to soak up the flavors of the dish and maintain their texture.

Summer squash love a quick blast from a hot grill because they'll cook before going soggy. Sautéing is another easy way to bring out sweetness. Chop the squash fairly small for fast cooking, and don't be afraid to let it get well browned and caramelized for deeper flavor. This brings me to another simple way to prepare summer squash—braised in a few glugs of good olive oil at a low temperature for a long period of time, then finished with fresh herbs. We often worry about overcooking vegetables, but extended cooking times can actually bring out their true vegetal flavor and a texture that nearly melts in your mouth.

In recent years, summer squash "noodles" have become very popular, showing up on many restaurant menus and in recipes galore published in magazines and on food blogs. Hailed as a pasta substitute, a plateful of squash noodles lacks the calories, carbs, or gluten of traditional noodles. They're quite refreshing and light, precisely what our bodies crave on hot, steamy days. Here are some options for creating noodles and ribbons, with or without fancy equipment.

To create ribbons: Rinse the squash, then trim off both ends. Using a sharp vegetable peeler, remove the skin and discard. Aiming for about half-inch-wide strips, begin peeling vertically and turning the squash as you go so the size of the strips stays consistent. Keep peeling until you hit the seeds and rough inner core. What's left is a pile of beautiful squash ribbons.

To create noodles: Following the same technique as above, use a julienne peeler instead of a traditional peeler once you have the outer skin removed. A mandoline slicer with the julienne blade attached is another option that gives more control and a steadier surface. If you really want to get fancy, buy a machine that spiralizes vegetables, yielding perfect noodles in a matter of seconds.

ONE EASY DISH: Toss sautéed or grilled squash with beans or steamed grains, a generous handful of herbs, and a flavorful cheese like goat or feta. Finish with a squeeze of fresh lemon, and you've got a customized main dish salad.

NUTRITION: FIVE REASONS TO EAT SUMMER SQUASH

1. Summer squash are a rich source of magnesium, fiber, folate, riboflavin, phosphorus, potassium, and vitamins A, B_6, and C. Many of these nutrients have been shown to be helpful in the prevention of atherosclerosis and diabetic heart disease.
2. Summer squash are particularly high in concentrations of lutein, which helps prevent the onset of cataracts and macular degeneration.
3. Summer squash are high in manganese, a mineral that helps the body process fats, carbohydrates, and glucose to keep high cholesterol at bay.
4. Summer squash aren't technically a "superfood," but they contain antioxidants that protect against free radicals. They also contain beta carotene, a great source of protection from pollutants and chemicals that lead to cancer.
5. Not only is summer squash a nutrient-dense food, but one cup contains just thirty calories, mostly because it is 90 percent water. There are many different ways to enjoy it, so feel free to build it into your healthy eating repertoire.

Zucchini with edible blossom attached

LAYERED GREEK TZATZIKI DIP

In this dip, a slew of colorful vegetables are marinated with olive oil and garlic, then layered with cool, creamy tzatziki sauce, the well-known Greek condiment for gyros. You can use any herbs you like, but I prefer dill, parsley, and a little basil. Inspired by the beauty of seasonal produce, this healthy and refreshing dip is the perfect complement to grilled chicken or baby back ribs. If you're the one hosting, make this dip a day ahead to save time and to allow the flavors to deepen. **SERVES 8–10 AS AN APPETIZER**

MARINATED VEGETABLES

- 1 cup finely chopped zucchini
- 1 cup finely chopped cucumber
- ½ cup chopped canned artichokes
- 1½ cups chopped cherry tomatoes
- ¼ cup pitted, chopped kalamata olives
- 2 tablespoons olive oil
- 2 cloves garlic, minced
- 2 tablespoons chopped fresh basil
- ¼ teaspoon kosher salt
- ¼ teaspoon black pepper

DIP

zest and juice of 1 lemon

16 ounces light sour cream

½ cup Greek yogurt

¼ cup chopped fresh parsley

¼ cup chopped fresh dill

2 cloves garlic, minced

½ teaspoon kosher salt

¼ teaspoon black pepper

toasted pita wedges or tortilla chips for serving

....

Mix together all marinated vegetable ingredients and let sit at least 1 hour or overnight.

When ready to assemble, drain any liquid that has been drawn out of the vegetables. Measure out ¼ cup vegetables and set aside. Mix together dip ingredients. In a clear, round serving bowl, place about 1½ cups of vegetables, then top with about 1 cup of dip. Repeat layers, then place reserved vegetables in a circular mound on top. Alternatively, if you are short on time, forgo the layers and mix dip in with the marinated vegetables. Serve with toasted pita wedges or tortilla chips. ◊

SUMMER SQUASH AND PEACH KISSES

There isn't a much more adorable appetizer than these rolled-up "kisses" of summer. At your next summer party they'll lure in guests, curious to see what these tempting bites are all about. Creamy ricotta, slivered peaches, and basil leaves make an easy and fresh filling that's elegant without being complicated. If you don't care for ricotta, goat cheese would work, too: just be sure to let it soften so it's easier to mix. **MAKES ABOUT 18 KISSES**

2–3 medium zucchini or yellow squash

5 ounces full-fat ricotta cheese

zest and juice of ½ lemon

½ teaspoon olive oil

kosher salt

black pepper

2 peaches, peeled and thinly sliced

20–30 leaves fresh basil

Rinse zucchini, then slice off top and bottom so you have flat surfaces. Use a mandoline slicer or very sharp peeler to cut zucchini lengthwise into thin slices, about ¹⁄₁₆ of an inch if possible. Pat dry with paper towels. Combine ricotta, lemon zest and juice, olive oil, and salt and pepper to taste, mixing well. Spoon a heaping teaspoon of ricotta mixture into the center of each zucchini slice and spread it out evenly. Leave a little space at the narrowest end, as the mixture will spread a bit when you roll it up. At one end of the strip, place a slice of peach and 1 to 2 basil leaves. Roll up zucchini strips and place seam-side down on a platter. Serve chilled. ◊

ZATAR-SPICED PARMESAN ZUCCHINI CRISPS

A fresh-from-the-garden tomato soup on a rain-soaked summer day is just as comforting to me as a hearty bowl of chili in January. To go with my soup, I like to make Parmesan cheese crisps, a tasty gluten-free option that calls to mind the classic grilled cheese combo I grew up with. On a whim I decided to grate half a zucchini to add to the Parmesan shreds, and these lacey, cheesy vegetable crisps were born. The addition of zatar, a Middle Eastern spice blend with rosemary, sumac, and oregano, makes them extra special. As you spoon the mixture onto the baking sheet, err on the side of making the mounds quite thin; too thick, and the "crisps" will end up chewy rather than crispy. **MAKES ABOUT 20 CRISPS**

- ½ cup zucchini shredded using coarse blade of a food processor
- 1 cup shredded Parmesan cheese
- ½ teaspoon olive oil
- 1½ teaspoons zatar seasoning (or Italian seasoning)

Preheat oven to 375 degrees. Wrap zucchini in a paper towel and squeeze out excess moisture. Mix together all ingredients and drop spoonfuls of the mixture on a baking sheet covered with parchment paper or a Silpat mat. Gently flatten each mound with your finger and spread out a bit like snowflakes, leaving a little room in between the cheese shreds. This is the key to getting them thin and crispy. As the Parmesan melts, it will hold the crisps together.

Bake for about 8 minutes. The crisps should be sizzling and golden brown when you remove them from the oven. Allow crisps to settle on baking sheet for about 5 minutes, then transfer to a serving plate using a spatula. Crisps will firm up as they cool. ◇

STUFFED SQUASH BLOSSOMS WITH BURRATA AND CAPERS

Edible flowers have always intrigued me, especially when they're from a vegetable. Bright yellow squash blossoms start appearing in the markets early in the summer, bold and beautiful like Easter daffodils. You'll often see recipes for frying them, but I think that treatment overpowers their delicate, slightly herbal flavor. Gooey burrata cheese is the perfect filling for this fresh version since it doesn't need heat to soften. With salty capers and fresh lemon zest to accent, this is one gorgeously simple appetizer. **SERVES 4**

10 squash blossoms

12 ounces burrata

zest of 1 lemon

2 tablespoons minced capers

olive oil

flaky sea salt (Maldon)

Open the blossoms wide and brush away any dirt. Inside each blossom place a dollop of burrata, then dot with lemon zest and capers. Close the petals around the stuffing by twisting the top ends. Lay flat on a serving platter and brush with olive oil. Sprinkle with flaky sea salt and enjoy. ✧

BUMPER CROP SPICY SQUASH PICKLES

While technically a condiment, these spicy, sweet-and-sour squash pickles are a summer picnic staple in my house. Crisp and tasty on sandwiches, they're a nice addition to a cheese plate or even just plopped onto buttered bread. Made using the simple refrigerator method, these pickles are ready to eat in just a few hours, although their flavors really deepen if you can stand to wait a day or two. Next time you find yourself with a bumper crop of squash, this recipe will be your saving grace. **MAKES 3 PINTS**

9	sprigs cilantro
3	cloves garlic, halved
3	teaspoons mixed peppercorns
1½	teaspoons coriander seeds, divided
3	teaspoons red pepper flakes, crushed
1½	pounds yellow squash and zucchini
⅓	cup thinly sliced sweet onion
1¼	cups apple cider vinegar
1¼	cups water
2	teaspoons kosher salt
2½	tablespoons honey

Place the following in each of 3 pint-size jars: 3 sprigs cilantro, 2 halves garlic, 1 teaspoon peppercorns, ½ teaspoon coriander, and 1 teaspoon red pepper flakes. Set aside. Using a mandoline or very sharp knife, thinly slice the zucchini and squash into rounds. Toss with onion, then divide evenly into jars, packing tightly. In a small saucepan, bring vinegar, water, salt, and honey to a boil. Pour mixture into each jar, pressing down on vegetables so that brine covers them completely. Let cool completely. Cover and refrigerate for at least 4 hours; waiting 2 days to eat will result in maximum flavor. Will keep in refrigerator for 2 months. ◇

BABZINNI GANOUSH

You've probably heard of baba ganoush, the creamy Middle Eastern dip consisting of smoky, grilled eggplant pureed with tahini and fresh lemon juice. I took the same approach with zucchini, grilling until it charred and the flesh collapsed. After a spin in the food processor, this mysteriously addicting spread became a new hit. Blend in fresh herbs or your favorite spices to customize, then top with cherry tomatoes and a drizzle of olive oil for a stunning presentation. **SERVES 6 AS AN APPETIZER**

2½ pounds zucchini (about 3 large)

3 tablespoons olive oil, divided

2 cloves garlic, minced

3 tablespoons tahini (sesame seed paste)

juice of 1 lemon

½ teaspoon kosher salt

¼ teaspoon smoked paprika or cumin

fresh parsley for garnish

Preheat grill to medium-high (about 450 degrees). Rub zucchini with 1 tablespoon olive oil, then set directly onto grill. Roast for about 20 to 25 minutes, turning a few times, until skin is browned and a little charred. Pierce with a fork or knife to ensure the insides are soft. Remove from heat, let cool 10 minutes, then carefully slice in half lengthwise. Scrape the insides into a colander and let sit for 20 minutes to drain; set aside charred skin of 1 zucchini. In a food processor puree the zucchini flesh, skin of 1 zucchini, remaining 2 tablespoons olive oil, garlic, tahini, lemon juice, salt, and paprika until smooth. Taste and season with additional salt and lemon juice, if necessary. The mixture will be a bit runny: refrigerate for an hour or so to thicken. To serve, garnish with fresh parsley and an additional drizzle of olive oil. Will keep in refrigerator for 5 days. ◇

CSA Pico Guacamole

Ever end up with a single tomato, a few cucumbers, mystery peppers, and who knows what else lurking at the bottom of your CSA box? Instead of letting the lone soldiers go to waste, I chop them all up along with cubes of creamy avocado and plenty of tangy lime juice to create a hodgepodge pico de gallo. This recipe is just a base: feel free to experiment with whatever you have on hand throughout the seasons. Who knows: the texture and flavor combination you create might just become your new favorite. **MAKES 2–3 CUPS**

zucchini or yellow squash, finely chopped

tomatoes, seeded and finely chopped

cucumbers, seeded and finely chopped

kosher salt

onions, finely chopped

jalapeños, minced

radishes, finely chopped

2 cloves garlic, minced

cilantro, minced

fresh lime juice

avocado, peeled and cubed

Combine watery vegetables like zucchini, tomato, and cucumbers with a big pinch of salt and set in a strainer for 20 minutes to an hour to drain excess water. (Push around with a fork a few times to help the process along.) Once drained, combine vegetables with remaining ingredients, adding lime juice and additional salt to taste. Serve with tortilla chips, over grilled meats, or folded into an omelet. ◇

FLUFFY LEMON POPPY SEED SUMMER SQUASH PANCAKES

A burst of Sunday morning sunshine is matched by a burst of flavor in these fluffy, lemony pancakes with strands of yellow summer squash scattered throughout. The crunch from the poppy seeds is a great texture builder, kind of like nuts in baked goods. These cakes are plush inside with a lightly crisped edge; they smell heavenly and take well to a drizzle of maple syrup and fresh blueberries for good measure. If you like thinner pancakes that cook through a little quicker, use the larger amount of milk. The lesser amount will result in thicker, taller cakes of lemon joy. **MAKES 6 PANCAKES**

1 cup all-purpose flour (or 135 grams all-purpose gluten-free flour mix; see pages 9–10)

1 teaspoon baking powder

pinch kosher salt

½–¾ cup milk (dairy or nondairy; see head note)

3 tablespoons sugar

1 large egg

½ teaspoon vanilla

3 tablespoons fresh lemon juice, plus zest of 1 lemon

1 tablespoon olive oil

1 cup grated yellow squash, squeezed in paper towel to remove excess liquid

1 tablespoon poppy seeds

butter

blueberries and maple syrup for serving

In a large bowl, whisk together flour, baking powder, and salt. Set aside. In a separate bowl, whisk together milk, sugar, egg, vanilla, lemon juice, and olive oil. Stir in squash and lemon zest. Pour the wet ingredients all at once into the dry ingredients. Add the poppy seeds and stir just to combine. If the mixture seems dry, add a little more milk. Let the batter rest for 5 to 10 minutes.

Place a griddle or a nonstick pan over medium heat. Add a bit of butter or cooking spray. For each cake, pour ⅓ cup of batter onto hot pan. Cook until golden brown on the bottom and bubbling on top, about 2 minutes. Flip once and cook until golden brown on bottom, about 3 more minutes. Serve with a pat of butter and fresh blueberries or a drizzle of Minnesota maple syrup. ◊

Banana Oat Streusel Summer Squash Muffins

Banana Oat Streusel Summer Squash Muffins

Grated yellow squash and ripe bananas add moisture to these muffins, ensuring they are soft, tender, and full of nutrition. Humble, hearty oats offer a bit of heft to the crunchy streusel topping. I like to use grated yellow squash in this recipe so the color blends into the golden hue of the muffin, but zucchini will work, too; just peel it to avoid the tell-tale green flecks. For a healthy "on the go" breakfast, individually freeze these muffins and warm up in the microwave on your way out the door. **MAKES 12 MUFFINS**

1½ cups all-purpose flour (or 210 grams all-purpose gluten-free flour mix; see pages 9–10)

½ cup old-fashioned oats

1 teaspoon baking soda

¾ teaspoon cinnamon

¼ teaspoon kosher salt

1 large egg

½ cup lightly packed brown sugar

4 tablespoons (½ stick) unsalted butter, melted and cooled

2 tablespoons milk

1½ teaspoons vanilla

1 cup yellow squash, grated using the coarse holes on a box grater (see head note)

1 cup mashed, very ripe bananas (about 2 bananas)

STREUSEL

3 tablespoons old-fashioned oats

1 tablespoon lightly packed brown sugar

1 tablespoon all-purpose flour (or 9 grams all-purpose gluten-free flour mix; see pages 9–10)

3 tablespoons finely chopped pecans or almonds

1 tablespoon butter, melted

....

Preheat oven to 350 degrees. Prepare muffin pan with liners or spray well with nonstick cooking spray. In large bowl, whisk together flour, oats, baking soda, cinnamon, and salt. Set aside. In another large bowl, whisk together egg and brown sugar until no lumps remain. Stir in butter, milk, and vanilla. Then stir in squash and banana. Gradually add dry ingredients to wet, stirring until just combined and no specks of flour remain; do not over-mix. Fill each muffin cup about two-thirds full. In small bowl, combine streusel ingredients and sprinkle about ½ tablespoon onto top of each muffin. Bake for 20 minutes, until tops are slightly golden brown and wooden pick comes out clean. ◇

SOUTHWESTERN ZUCCHINI FRITTATA

Can't quite conquer the pesky step of flipping an omelet? Say hello to its Italian cousin the frittata, in which whisked eggs are cooked over low heat, then baked until golden brown. Brightened with fresh cilantro, salty feta, and a little sriracha kick, the mild, delicate zucchini is elevated by the corn's sweetness. Filled with a combination of vegetables that scream summer and ready to serve in fewer than thirty minutes, this version is one of my go-to brunch plates. **SERVES 4**

    7 large eggs
    ¼ cup milk
    ¼ cup chopped cilantro, plus more for garnish
    ½ teaspoon kosher salt
    ¼ teaspoon black pepper
    ½ cup crumbled feta
    1½ tablespoons butter
    ¾ cup grilled sweet corn kernels
        (or frozen sweet corn, thawed)
    ⅓ cup chopped green onions, white and green parts
    ⅓ cup chopped roasted red peppers
    1 small zucchini, thinly sliced into eighth-inch rounds
    sriracha

Preheat oven to 375 degrees. In a large mixing bowl lightly whisk together eggs, milk, cilantro, salt, and pepper. Stir in feta and set aside. Set a large cast-iron skillet or ovenproof nonstick skillet over medium heat. Melt butter in pan and swirl so it coats bottom and partially up the sides. Add corn, onions, and peppers and cook, stirring, for 2 minutes. Pour egg mixture over vegetables and cook until just beginning to set, about 2 minutes. Remove from heat and scatter zucchini slices in a circular pattern on top. Place skillet in oven and bake about 10 minutes, until frittata is just set in the middle, puffed around the sides, and lightly golden. Slice and serve garnished with extra cilantro and sriracha (or your favorite hot sauce). Will keep in refrigerator for 2 days. ◇

Sweet Corn and Summer Squash Vichyssoise

This soup has the golden hue of the sun from three different yellow vegetables: slender summer squash, young sweet corn, and crisp yellow bell peppers. For the most robust flavor, grab just-picked corn from a farmers market or roadside country stand. The buttery broth comes from boiling the cobs with the rest of the ingredients to create a "corn milk." No cream is needed; just a touch of Greek yogurt will do. Served with a simple green salad, this vichyssoise becomes a lovely lunchtime meal that's sure to brighten your day. **SERVES 4 AS A MAIN DISH OR 6 AS A FIRST COURSE**

1½ tablespoons butter

1 clove garlic, minced

1 cup chopped onion

kosher salt

1 heaping cup coarsely chopped yellow squash

2½ cups raw sweet corn, cut from about 4 ears; reserve 3 cobs

½ cup chopped yellow bell pepper

1 medium potato, peeled and chopped

½ teaspoon smoked paprika

¼ teaspoon cayenne

¼ teaspoon black pepper

3 cups low-sodium vegetable broth

2 tablespoons nonfat Greek yogurt

3 tablespoons fresh lime juice

minced cilantro for garnish

In large stockpot, melt butter over medium heat. Add garlic and cook, stirring, for 1 minute. Add onion and pinch of salt. Cook, stirring, about 5 minutes, until softened. Stir in squash, corn, bell pepper, potato, another pinch of salt, smoked paprika, cayenne, and black pepper. Cook for about

3 minutes, then add vegetable broth and 3 corn cobs. Bring to a boil, then partially cover and cook for 20 minutes or until all vegetables are softened. Remove from heat and discard cobs. Stir in yogurt and lime juice. Working in batches, puree in a food processor until completely smooth. Add more salt or cayenne to taste. Garnish with cilantro and serve. ◇

Minted Pea and Zucchini Soup with Crème Fraîche

Nothing beats a refreshing chilled soup on a sweltering, humid day. This vibrant green summertime starter is a silky puree of sweet peas and zucchini, perked up with fresh mint. After you've chopped the zucchini, this soup comes together in just fifteen minutes, then chills for an hour. A swirl of crème fraîche gives a hit of tanginess, a delightful complement to sweet seasonal flavors. **SERVES 4 AS A FIRST COURSE**

....

10	ounces sweet peas (fresh or frozen, thawed)
1	tablespoon olive oil
¼	cup chopped green onion, white and green parts
	kosher salt
1	cup coarsely chopped zucchini
1½	cups low-sodium vegetable broth
¼	cup milk (dairy or unsweetened nondairy)
¾	cup loosely packed mint leaves
¼	teaspoon black pepper
½	teaspoon apple cider vinegar
	crème fraîche (or plain yogurt) for serving

....

Pour peas into a high-powered blender. In skillet, heat oil over medium heat. Add onion and big pinch of salt, and cook, stirring, for 1 to 2 minutes. Add zucchini and cook, stirring, for another 5 minutes. Stir in broth and milk, then bring to a simmer. Remove from heat; add mixture to blender. Blend on high power for 1 minute. Add in mint leaves, ¾ teaspoon salt, pepper, and vinegar. Blend for 1 to 2 minutes, until completely smooth. Adjust salt to taste. Chill soup for at least 1 hour before serving. To serve, place in bowls and top with a tablespoon of crème fraîche. ◊

Caprese Zucchini Noodle Salad

Sorry, spaghetti: I think I've broken up with you for the summer after discovering how to turn zucchini into tender, pastalike "noodles." Highlighting one of the classic salads of summer, this recipe is raw, vegetarian, and seriously good. The cherry tomatoes and mini mozzarella balls make a beautiful presentation, all while absorbing the garlicky balsamic dressing. Great right after everything is tossed together, but even better after thirty minutes of marinating in the refrigerator. **SERVES 3–4 AS A SIDE DISH**

....

SALAD

2 pounds long and slender summer squash
  (yellow and zucchini)

kosher salt

10 mini mozzarella balls, halved

1 pint cherry tomatoes, halved

¼ cup loosely packed basil leaves, thinly sliced,
  plus more for garnish

DRESSING

3 tablespoons olive oil

1 tablespoon balsamic vinegar

¼ teaspoon Dijon-style mustard

2 cloves garlic, minced

½ teaspoon kosher salt

¼ teaspoon black pepper

....

\>>

Create raw "noodles" from the squash using mandoline slicer or julienne peeler (see page 15). Place in colander, toss with ¼ teaspoon salt, and let sit for 20 minutes. Roll up noodles in middle of kitchen towel like you would the filling for a burrito. Wring towel to remove water from noodles. In large bowl, toss together zucchini, mozzarella, tomatoes, and basil. In separate bowl, whisk together dressing ingredients; pour over vegetables, and toss to combine. Chill for 20 minutes, then garnish with extra basil and enjoy. ◇

SESAME-GINGER FORBIDDEN BLACK RICE SALAD

Forbidden black rice, available at co-ops or in the Asian section of larger grocery stores, is an heirloom grain treasured for its roasted nutty taste and soft texture. It turns a beautiful deep purple when cooked and provides the highest level of vitamins, minerals, and fiber of any bran rice. In this salad the grains are combined with crunchy zucchini and other summer vegetables, then coated in a lively sesame-ginger dressing. Serve with a glass of Torrontés or fruity white wine for a mouth-pleasing pairing. **SERVES 6–8 AS A SIDE DISH**

1 cup forbidden black rice (or wild or brown rice)

DRESSING

2 tablespoons sesame oil

1½ tablespoons olive oil

2 cloves garlic, minced

2 tablespoons freshly grated ginger

1 tablespoon honey

¼ cup rice vinegar

2 tablespoons tamari (or soy sauce)

½ teaspoon kosher salt

SALAD

1½ cups sugar snap peas, trimmed and halved diagonally

1 cup finely chopped zucchini

2 green onions, white and green parts, thinly sliced

¾ cup grated carrots

¼ cup chopped fresh basil

2 tablespoons chopped fresh mint

½ cup sunflower seeds

....

Place black rice in a strainer and rinse thoroughly, swishing to remove extra starch, until water runs mostly clear. Add rice to medium pot and cover with 4 inches of water. Add big pinch of salt and bring to a boil. Reduce heat to simmer and cook rice for about 45 minutes, until al dente. (The water will turn a purplish hue.) Drain and rinse with cold water; set aside to cool.

While rice is cooking, whisk together dressing ingredients and set aside. When rice has cooled, combine with the vegetables and herbs in large bowl. Stir in dressing and top with sunflower seeds. Serve chilled or at room temperature. Will keep in refrigerator for up to 4 days. ◇

EASY CURRIED TOFU SALAD

This vegetarian and Indian-inspired play on classic chicken salad is delightful when stuffed into a toasted pita or piled onto a bed of crisp salad greens. The crunch from the zucchini and celery play off the creamy texture of the tofu, and zesty curry powder lights up the palate. It pays to make this dish in advance so the flavors can meld.

For best results, remove the tofu from its package, pat it dry, and wrap it in paper towels. Place wrapped tofu in a baking pan, set a cast-iron skillet (or other heavy object) on top, and let sit for 20 minutes to press out as much water as possible. If tofu isn't on your radar (although I think you'll love it if you try it in this recipe), chicken would be a great substitute. **SERVES 4**

8 ounces extra-firm tofu, drained and pressed (see head note), cut into one-inch cubes

¼ cup chopped celery

¾ cup halved green grapes

1 cup finely chopped zucchini

¼ cup mayonnaise

¼ cup nonfat plain yogurt

1 teaspoon curry powder

¼ teaspoon cumin

½ teaspoon kosher salt

pinch cayenne

2 tablespoons chopped cilantro

Place tofu, celery, grapes, and zucchini in large bowl. In separate smaller bowl, whisk together remaining ingredients. Add dressing to bowl with vegetables and stir gently to combine. Taste and add more salt if desired. Will keep in refrigerator for up to 4 days. ◇

PUNCHY PESTO PASTA SALAD

This recipe can be ready at a moment's notice thanks to a jar of prepared pesto and a can of white beans. The zucchini adds freshness, and the arugula provides a peppery bite. Dished up alongside grilled pork chops or chicken, this salad's seasonal flavors simply shine. If you're looking for a crowd-pleasing dish that's easy to prepare and packed with nutrition, this one's for you. **SERVES 8**

8 ounces cavatappi or penne pasta
   (gluten free if desired; Tinkyada brand)

1 (7-ounce) jar good-quality pesto (or make your own)

¼ cup red wine vinegar

½ teaspoon kosher salt

1 (15-ounce) can kidney beans, rinsed and drained

3 cups (about 2½ ounces) arugula

1 small zucchini, halved lengthwise and thinly sliced
   (about 1 cup)

¼ cup thinly sliced red onion

2 ounces Parmesan cheese, shaved (about ½ cup), divided

Cook pasta according to package directions, making sure to add a big pinch of salt to the water. Drain and rinse well under *cold* water. In a large bowl, stir together pesto, vinegar, and salt. Add beans, arugula, zucchini, red onion, cooked pasta, and half of cheese to pesto mixture, folding to combine. Transfer to serving bowl and top with remaining cheese. Serve at room temperature. Will keep in refrigerator for 2 days. ◇

REFRESHING SUMMER SQUASH AND WATERMELON SALAD

I equate this refreshing salad to the thirst quencher that agua fresca can be. When it's so hot you can't even think about heating up the stove, this beautiful pile of veggie noodles and cool watermelon is the answer. It's hydrating and crunchy, sprinkled with a confetti of red pepper flakes and fresh herbs to make your tongue tingle. Drop this tangle onto a sea-salted wedge of crisp melon for a shockingly delicious summer beauty. **SERVES 2**

Refreshing Summer Squash and Watermelon Salad

  1 tablespoon sesame seeds

1½ tablespoons fresh lemon juice

1½ tablespoons olive oil

 ¼ teaspoon kosher salt

  1 tablespoon chopped fresh mint

  1 tablespoon chopped cilantro

  2 small yellow squash (the straighter the better), about 1¼ pounds

  1 (1½ –inch) piece watermelon, cut into 4 wedges

  2 tablespoons sunflower seeds

     red pepper flakes

....

In a skillet, toast sesame seeds over medium-high heat, shaking the pan occasionally, about 3 to 4 minutes, being careful not to let them burn. When they are fragrant, remove from heat and empty onto a plate to cool. In a small bowl, whisk together lemon juice, olive oil, salt, and herbs. Set aside.

Cut stems and bottom inch off of squash. Create squash noodles by using a mandoline or a julienne vegetable peeler (see page 15). Toss the noodles with the dressing; taste and add salt if needed. Lay two slices of watermelon on each plate, with tips of triangles touching. Distribute noodles evenly on both plates, mounding atop watermelon. Sprinkle each plate with sunflower seeds and sesame seeds, then garnish with red pepper flakes. ◇

TOMATO AND SUMMER SQUASH COBBLER WITH ROSEMARY BISCUITS

As sweet as sun-ripened cherry tomatoes are right off the vine, they become even more so when baked with layers of summer squash in this savory cobbler-style dish. Fresh thyme, garlic, and onion balance the dish, and biscuits studded with rosemary and feta top it all off. For fluffy and tender biscuits, be sure to not over-mix, but don't worry about making them perfectly round. Being perfectly imperfect never hurt anyone. **SERVES 4**

BISCUITS

2 cups all-purpose flour (or 280 grams all-purpose gluten-free flour mix; see pages 9–10)

2 tablespoons baking powder

1½ tablespoons minced fresh rosemary (or ½ tablespoon dried)

½ teaspoon sugar

¾ teaspoon kosher salt

¼ teaspoon black pepper

6 tablespoons (¾ stick) unsalted butter, chilled and cut into one-inch cubes

½ cup crumbled feta cheese

¾ cup buttermilk, plus more for topping

FILLING

2½ tablespoons olive oil, divided

½ large onion, thinly sliced

¾ teaspoon kosher salt, divided

2 cloves garlic, minced

1 pint cherry tomatoes

1½ pounds summer squash (yellow and zucchini),
thinly sliced into rounds

1 tablespoon all-purpose flour (or 1 tablespoon all-purpose
gluten-free flour mix; see pages 9–10)

1 tablespoon minced fresh thyme (or ½ tablespoon dried)

¼ teaspoon black pepper

....

In a medium bowl, whisk together flour, baking powder, rosemary, sugar, salt, and pepper. Add cold butter. With your fingers or a pastry blender, rub butter into dry ingredients until well incorporated and butter is the size of small peas. Toss in feta, stirring to incorporate. Create a small well in the center of the flour mixture. Add buttermilk and bring together all the ingredients with a fork. The dough will be rather shaggy. Dump dough onto a lightly floured work surface and lightly knead until it comes together. Wrap dough in plastic wrap and refrigerate until the filling is assembled.

To make the filling, preheat oven to 375 degrees. Coat an 8x8– or 9x9–inch pan with nonstick spray and set aside. Add 1 tablespoon olive oil to a medium skillet set over medium heat. Add onion and ¼ teaspoon salt. Cook onion, stirring occasionally, until caramelized, about 15 minutes. Add garlic and cook for 1 minute, then remove from heat and pour into prepared dish. Set aside.

In a large bowl, toss together tomatoes, squash, remaining 1½ tablespoons olive oil, flour, and thyme. Season with pepper and remaining ½ teaspoon salt. Distribute mixture evenly over onions, and bake filling for 25 minutes.

Meanwhile, remove biscuit dough from the fridge. On a lightly floured work surface, roll into a ¾ or 1-inch thickness, and cut 6 biscuits with a round biscuit cutter. (Excess dough can be cut into rounds and frozen, then baked at another time.) Remove partially cooked filling from oven and place biscuits on top. Brush biscuits with extra buttermilk and add a sprinkle of salt. Return pan to oven and bake for 15 to 20 minutes, until biscuits are golden brown and cooked through and tomato mixture is bubbling. Remove from oven and allow to cool for about 10 minutes before serving. ◇

ZUCCHINI, ARTICHOKE, AND ROASTED RED PEPPER RISOTTO

Risotto sings the true essence of comfort any time of year, and this one, plumb full of summer vegetables and fresh basil, does not disappoint. Beaming with a rainbow of colors, it's a vegetarian and naturally gluten-free dish that's amazingly rich and creamy. The flavors are bright and herbal, the paper-thin zucchini nearly melting into the rice. One of the perks of risotto is its adaptability to the seasons or whatever your CSA box surprises you with, so feel free to improvise. **SERVES 4**

1 tablespoon olive oil

2 cloves garlic, minced

½ cup finely chopped onion

1¼ cups Arborio rice

1 (7.5-ounce) jar marinated artichokes, liquid reserved, artichokes drained and chopped

½ cup dry white wine

4½ cups low-sodium vegetable broth, warmed, plus more as needed

½ teaspoon dried thyme

½ teaspoon kosher salt

¼ teaspoon black pepper

1 small zucchini and 1 small yellow squash, halved lengthwise and thinly sliced into half moons (about 1–1½ cups)

⅓ cup finely chopped red bell peppers

⅓ cup freshly grated Parmesan cheese

2 tablespoons butter

¼ cup chopped fresh basil

In a large saucepan over medium heat, warm olive oil. Increase heat and add garlic and onion. Cook, stirring, until softened and fragrant, about 2 minutes. Add rice and reserved artichoke liquid and cook, stirring, until rice is translucent with a white spot in the middle, looking somewhat like a tooth, about 3 to 4 minutes. Add wine and cook, stirring, until completely absorbed, about 1 minute. Add 1 cup warm stock, thyme, salt, and pepper. Cook over moderate heat, stirring, until nearly absorbed. Add another cup of stock and stir until it is absorbed. Stir in squash, artichokes, and red peppers. Add remaining stock, 1 cup at a time, stirring between additions until almost completely absorbed. Test the rice to see if it is al dente, and if not, add more stock by the half cup and cook until rice reaches desired texture, usually 25 to 30 minutes. It should be creamy with a toothsome bite. Stir in the cheese, butter, and basil and, once melted, remove from heat. Season with additional salt and pepper as desired. ◇

Zucchini, Artichoke, and Roasted Red Pepper Risotto

Cherry Tomato, Zucchini, and Blue Cheese Galette

Are you like me and intimidated by making a pie crust? Have no fear: the imperfect but elegant galette is just the answer, with hand-folded edges and no pan needed. Jagged corners of buttery cornmeal crust encase thinly sliced zucchini and seared cherry tomatoes. I adapted this recipe from one of my favorite food writers, Deb Perelman of Smitten Kitchen, who had the brilliant idea to lightly char the tomatoes in a sizzling pan until they burst. This step concentrates their flavor while getting rid of excess moisture to prevent a soggy crust. Serve this galette with fresh greens and a bottle of Sauvignon Blanc for an al fresco dinner under the stars. **SERVES 2–3**

CRUST

1 cup cold all-purpose flour (or 140 grams all-purpose gluten-free flour mix; see pages 9–10)

⅓ cup cornmeal

¾ teaspoon kosher salt

7 tablespoons frozen unsalted butter, cut into small cubes

3–4 tablespoons ice-cold water

2 tablespoons ice-cold vodka (or 2 additional tablespoons ice-cold water)

FILLING

½ tablespoon olive oil, plus more for finishing

1 pound cherry tomatoes

kosher salt

2 cloves garlic, thinly sliced

1 small zucchini, sliced into eighth-inch rounds (about 1 cup)

black pepper

3½ ounces creamy blue cheese, crumbled

2 tablespoons thinly sliced basil

To prepare pastry, combine flour, cornmeal, and salt in bowl of food processor; pulse two times. Add butter to flour mixture; pulse 4 to 5 times, until mixture has little clumps, like small peas. Add in 3 tablespoons water and the vodka, pulsing a few times until incorporated. Dough will be shaggy; it should not form a ball. Remove from food processor bowl and press mixture together into a ball as if packing a snowball. If necessary, add more ice-cold water, a tablespoon at a time, until it sticks together. Pat dough into a half-inch-thick round disk. Wrap tightly in plastic wrap, then refrigerate for at least 1 hour or up to 3 days. With floured rolling pin, roll out dough on parchment paper into an 11- to 12-inch circle (it doesn't have to be exact, this is rustic!).

Preheat oven to 375 degrees. To prepare filling, add olive oil, tomatoes, and ¼ teaspoon salt to skillet with a lid and place over medium-high heat. Cover and cook, shaking skillet a few times to roll tomatoes around. Continue shaking as you start to hear them sizzle and pop, lifting the lid every few minutes to check their progress. Once almost all have burst, remove from heat, stir in half of sliced garlic, and empty into a large bowl to cool mixture before assembling.

Transfer dough and parchment to baking sheet. In middle of rolled-out dough, create a circle of overlapping zucchini, one or two layers, leaving about 2½ inches to the border. Sprinkle with ¼ teaspoon salt and ¼ teaspoon pepper. Distribute remaining garlic evenly across zucchini, as well as half of blue cheese. Cover zucchini and blue cheese layer with tomatoes. Fold up edges of crust so that at least half of the tomatoes are encased by the dough. Bake for 30 minutes, then sprinkle with remaining blue cheese. Bake for another 5 to 10 minutes, until crust is browned. Remove from oven and brush crust with a little olive oil. Top with fresh basil, even putting some on the crust. Serve in slices. ◇

Cherry Tomato, Zucchini, and Blue Cheese Galette (page 46)

TEMPEH COCONUT GREEN CURRY

Tempeh, a vegetarian substitute like tofu, is famous for its nutty, hearty flavor and nougat-like texture. It works beautifully in curries because it absorbs the vibrant flavors from the spices and rich coconut milk. This fragrant one-pot meal is versatile in terms of vegetables and proteins, but I love using eggplant and zucchini for the silky texture they acquire after simmering in all of the curry goodness. If you don't have tempeh on hand, tofu or pork would work well, too. Finished with toasted coconut and crunchy peanuts, this inspired dish also makes great leftovers. **SERVES 5–6**

....

2 tablespoons coconut oil

2 cloves garlic, minced

1 medium red onion, cut into half-inch wedges

1½ teaspoons turmeric

2 tablespoons green curry paste (found in the Asian food section)

¾ teaspoon kosher salt

1 medium globe eggplant, skin on or peeled, cut into one-inch pieces

1 medium zucchini, halved lengthwise, then sliced into half moons

1½ cups yellow string beans halved crosswise

8 ounces tempeh, cut into one-inch cubes (or 1½ cups cooked, cubed pork or tofu)

1 (15-ounce) can coconut milk (light works, but I prefer full fat)

juice of 1 small lime

⅓ cup chopped fresh Thai basil

⅓ cup toasted, unsweetened coconut flakes

¼ cup crushed peanuts

cooked white rice or quinoa for serving

....

In a medium Dutch oven or large skillet, heat coconut oil over medium-high heat. Add garlic and onion and cook, stirring, for a few minutes until softened. Stir in turmeric, curry paste, and salt; cook for another 1 to 2 minutes, coating the onions and garlic with the spices. Add remaining vegetables and tempeh, stirring to combine. Pour in coconut milk and bring to a boil. Reduce heat to a simmer and cook, partially covered, for 20 to 25 minutes, until vegetables are tender, stirring occasionally. Remove from heat and stir in lime juice and basil. Taste and add more salt if needed. Garnish with coconut and crushed peanuts, then serve over rice or quinoa. Will keep in refrigerator for up to 4 days. ◇

ZUCCHINI CAULIFLOWER SUMMER GRATIN

There's much to be learned from iconic chefs such as one of my favorites, Julia Child. In one of her cookbooks, she mentioned squeezing the water out of grated, salted zucchini, then using the water as part of the simmering liquid (with cream, too, of course) when making a summer casserole. Taking her lead, I created this healthy zucchini cauliflower gratin. The zucchini liquid forms the base to a light béchamel, and the ricelike cauliflower soaks up any remaining juices. Baked until bubbly with a perfectly golden Parmesan topping, this irresistible gratin is one you'll be making all summer long. **SERVES 4 AS A SIDE DISH**

1	large head cauliflower
	kosher salt
1¼	pounds zucchini, coarsely grated
2	tablespoons olive oil
¾	cup chopped onion
2	cloves garlic, minced
½	teaspoon finely ground black pepper
2	tablespoons all-purpose flour (or 2 tablespoons gluten-free all-purpose flour mix; see pages 9–10)
¼	cup milk
⅓	cup heavy cream
⅔	cup grated Parmesan cheese, divided
1	tablespoon chopped fresh rosemary
3	tablespoons chopped fresh parsley

Tear leaves off the cauliflower and cut head in half. Cut florets off of core until you are left with just the core. Discard core and break up florets into smaller, somewhat uniform pieces. Working in batches, place florets into bowl of food processor and process until evenly chopped. The pieces should be fine like rice grains but not pulverized, yielding about 3½ cups.

Preheat oven to 375 degrees. Coat a shallow baking dish with nonstick spray and set aside. Stir 1 teaspoon salt and grated zucchini together, then place in colander set over a bowl to drain. In a large skillet, heat olive oil over medium-high heat, add onions and a big pinch of salt, and cook, stirring, until softened, about 4 to 5 minutes. Meanwhile, squeeze handfuls of the zucchini over a bowl to catch the juices, removing almost all of the water from the grated shreds, yielding about ⅔ cup shreds. Zucchini will still be damp, but the excess liquid will be out.

When onion is softened, reduce heat to medium and stir in cauliflower, garlic, zucchini, ½ teaspoon salt, and pepper. Cook for about 7 to 8 minutes, until vegetables are softened. Sprinkle flour over the mixture and stir to combine. Gradually stir in reserved zucchini water, milk, and cream, maintaining heat at medium so dairy does not curdle. Cook for 2 to 3 minutes so liquid slightly absorbs. Remove from heat. Stir in ⅓ cup cheese, rosemary, and parsley. Pour into prepared dish and bake for 20 minutes. Remove from oven and top with remaining ⅓ cup cheese (or more if you like). Return to oven for another 10 or so minutes, until gratin is brown and bubbly. ◇

Zucchini Cauliflower Summer Gratin (page 50)

BUFFALO CHICKEN ZUCCHINI MEATBALLS

Numerous orders of buffalo wings from my favorite local joint, the Blue Door Pub, have turned me into a hot sauce fanatic. Making wings in your own kitchen can be quite labor intensive and messy, so I created a meatball version instead. Zucchini, onions, and green peppers are mixed into ground chicken, making the meatballs flavor all-stars while keeping them incredibly juicy. As an added bonus in the health department, they're baked, not fried. Enjoy these easy buffalo chicken meatballs as a fun weeknight dinner, or prepare them a day ahead of time for a no-fuss party appetizer. **SERVES 3–4**

1 large egg white

⅔ cup coarsely grated zucchini, squeezed in paper towel to remove excess liquid

¼ cup finely chopped green bell pepper

2 tablespoons minced white onion

1 clove garlic, minced

¼ teaspoon celery salt

¼ teaspoon kosher salt

pinch black pepper

½ cup plus 1 tablespoon panko breadcrumbs (or gluten-free breadcrumbs or quinoa flakes)

1 pound ground chicken (or ground turkey)

2 tablespoons butter

½ cup Frank's Hot Sauce (or your favorite hot sauce)

cooked white rice

blue cheese

fresh parsley

\>\>

Preheat oven to 400 degrees. Coat baking sheet with nonstick cooking spray and set aside. In large bowl, stir together egg white, zucchini, green pepper, onion, garlic, celery salt, salt, pepper, and breadcrumbs with a fork. Add in chicken and mix to combine, being careful not to over-handle to keep meatballs from getting tough. Refrigerate mixture for 5 minutes, then roll into 10 firmly packed meatballs, about 2 inches in diameter. Place meatballs on prepared baking sheet and bake for 12 to 14 minutes. Test one to be sure they are cooked through. (If you are making this recipe ahead of time, stop at this point and refrigerate meatballs. When ready to serve, warm meatballs over low heat in a skillet and then continue the recipe.)

Melt butter in a skillet over medium heat, then add hot sauce and stir to combine. Add cooked meatballs to skillet and use a spoon to roll and fully coat them in the sauce. Remove with a slotted spoon and serve over rice. Top with additional sauce, crumbled blue cheese, and fresh parsley. ◇

Spicy Shakshuka

A gift of tomatoes and peppers during the peak of summer inspired me to give this traditional Middle Eastern dish some Mexican flair. Pronounced shak-shook-a, *this one-dish wonder features eggs nestled into a warming, spicy tomato sauce full of seasonal vegetables. Humble yet full of flavor from the adobo chili and spices, this meal is perfect any time of the day. Don't forget a warm crusty baguette to soak up every last bit of sauce.* **SERVES 4**

2 tablespoons olive oil

2 cloves garlic, minced

1 cup chopped onion

1 medium red bell pepper, finely chopped

1 cup finely chopped yellow squash or zucchini

1 teaspoon cumin

kosher salt

½ teaspoon chili powder

2 pounds tomatoes, roughly chopped,
   or 1 (28-ounce) can diced tomatoes

¼ cup water

1 tablespoon chopped chiles en adobo sauce

½ teaspoon black pepper

4 tablespoons chopped cilantro, divided

5–6 large eggs

¼ cup crumbled feta

toasted baguettes for serving

....

Heat oil in a large skillet over medium heat. Add garlic and onions and cook, stirring, for 2 minutes, until soft and fragrant. Add red peppers, squash, cumin, 1 teaspoon salt, and chili powder. Cook, stirring, for 5 minutes, until all vegetables are soft.

Stir in the tomatoes, water, chiles en adobo, and black pepper. Cook at a very low simmer until the tomatoes are crushed and thickened, about 20 minutes. Stir in 2 tablespoons cilantro. With back of a spoon, make 5 to 6 "wells" in the mixture and crack the eggs into these spots. Sprinkle eggs with a few pinches of salt. Increase heat to medium and cook, partially covered, for 6 to 8 minutes, until whites are set and yolks are thick. Sprinkle feta and remaining cilantro over top and serve with toasted baguette. ◇

Ultimate Grilled Veggie Tacos with Pepita Salsa

If there's one thing I love, it's a good dinner party. These vegetarian tacos have been a smashing hit with many of my guests. Marinated zucchini and yellow squash are grilled, then jazzed up with a pepita salsa that is similar to a pesto, yet heartier and spicier. The zip of pickled onions and the creaminess of goat cheese bring out the best in all of the ingredients. For even cooking and grill marks, be sure to cut squash into pickle-like spears. **SERVES 5–6**

SALSA

¾ cup raw pepita seeds

½ cup packed cilantro leaves and stems

1 roma tomato or 10 cherry tomatoes

1 teaspoon kosher salt

⅛ teaspoon cayenne, plus more to taste

⅓ cup water

TACOS

1 (15-ounce) can black beans, drained but not rinsed

1 teaspoon cumin, divided

kosher salt

4 tablespoons fresh lime juice, divided, plus more for garnish

1¼ pounds long and slender summer squash (yellow and zucchini)

1 clove garlic, minced

2 tablespoons olive oil

1 teaspoon chili powder

3 tablespoons chopped fresh basil

corn tortillas

goat cheese

pickled onions or minced red onions

For the salsa, heat a small skillet over medium-high heat. Add pepita seeds and cook, swirling pan often, until lightly toasted, about 3 minutes. Let cool for about 5 minutes, then add to bowl of food processor with all other salsa ingredients and process until mostly smooth. Taste and adjust seasonings as needed. Set aside.

In a small saucepan over medium heat, warm drained black beans with ½ teaspoon cumin, pinch of salt, and 2 tablespoons lime juice until heated through. Remove from heat and set aside.

Cut squash in half lengthwise, then into quarters, then crosswise to create pickle-size spears (see head note). In a small bowl, whisk together the remaining 2 tablespoons lime juice, garlic, olive oil, chili powder, remaining ½ teaspoon cumin, and ½ teaspoon salt. Put squash in large sealable plastic bag and pour in marinade. Seal bag and shake to fully coat. Refrigerate for 30 minutes.

Preheat grill on medium-high heat and grease grates with vegetable oil. Drain squash, reserving marinade. When grill is hot, cook squash for 4 minutes on each side, until grill marks are visible and squash is tender. Remove from heat and toss in leftover marinade with basil.

To assemble, spread 1½ tablespoons salsa into middle of tortilla. Spoon beans over salsa, add squash spears, then goat cheese, and finally the pickled onion. Squeeze with additional lime and enjoy. ◇

Garam Masala–Dusted Pattypans and Chickpeas with Tahini Sauce

Ever notice those yellow and green flying saucers situated next to the mountains of bell peppers at the farmers market in late July? Don't be fooled— they're just an innocent summer squash called the pattypan. Underneath their delicate skin (which doesn't need to be peeled), you'll find flesh the color of clotted cream with tiny edible seeds. I like to buy the tiniest ones I can find; they are buttery and subtly sweet rather than watery and bland like the larger ones. This deliciously quick and easy meatless dish is all about warming Indian spices sinking into roasted, itty-bitty squash and chickpeas. A drizzle of silky tahini, a sprinkle of fresh herbs, and after your first bite you'll know you've found a standby recipe for pattypans. **SERVES 4 AS A SIDE DISH**

....

SAUCE

¼ teaspoon kosher salt

1 clove garlic

1 tablespoon chopped cilantro

⅓ cup tahini (sesame seed paste)

1 tablespoon chopped fresh parsley

2 tablespoons olive oil

2 tablespoons fresh lemon juice

3 tablespoons water

SQUASH

1½ pounds baby pattypan squash
(about 1–2 inches in diameter)

1 medium to large red bell pepper, cut into half-inch squares

1 (15-ounce) can chickpeas (garbanzo beans),
drained and dried with a towel

3 tablespoons olive oil

2 teaspoons garam masala

½ teaspoon smoked paprika

1 teaspoon kosher salt

cilantro or parsley for garnish

....

To make sauce, place salt, garlic, and cilantro into bowl of food processor and process for 20 seconds. (The salt helps keep the garlic from sticking to the blade.) Add remaining sauce ingredients and process for 30 seconds. Scrape down sides of bowl, then process for another 30 seconds. Taste and add more salt if needed. Set aside.

Preheat oven to 400 degrees. If pattypans are wider than an inch in diameter, halve them. Place in a bowl with red pepper and chickpeas, then drizzle in olive oil and spices. Stir to fully coat and spread onto a large parchment paper–lined baking sheet or divide between two pans if one seems crowded. Roast for 25 to 30 minutes or until squash pierces easily with a fork.

To serve, mound vegetables on a plate and drizzle with tahini sauce. Garnish with cilantro or parsley. ◇

Garam Masala–Dusted Pattypans and Chickpeas (page 58)

CHIMICHURRI CHICKEN AND VEGETABLE KABOBS

Heat up the grill: we're having a kabob party! This recipe is all about the chimichurri, a mildly spicy, vinegar-laced pesto that is the quintessential sauce of Argentina. When fresh herbs are growing like weeds in your garden, whirl them into this flavor-packed marinade. Chimichurri's spicy, garlicky punch pairs well with the smokiness of grilled chicken and vegetables. And this sauce is extremely versatile: I sometimes make a double batch and use it during the week as a killer salad dressing. **SERVES 4**

CHIMICHURRI

2½   teaspoons kosher salt

3   cloves garlic, peeled

¾   cup loosely packed parsley

½   cup loosely packed cilantro

½ cup loosely packed basil

½ jalapeño, sliced

¼ cup apple cider vinegar or red wine vinegar

½ cup olive oil

KABOBS

Cut the following into 1-inch pieces:

1 pound boneless, skinless chicken breasts

1 large onion

1 small zucchini

1 small yellow squash

1 red bell pepper

wooden skewers

Greek yogurt or sour cream for serving (optional)

....

To make chimichurri, add salt and garlic to bowl of food processor (the salt helps keep the garlic from sticking to the blade). Process for 10 seconds, scrape down bowl, and run for 10 more seconds. Add in herbs and jalapeño. Process for 20 seconds or so, scrape down bowl, and repeat. With blade running, add vinegar, then slowly add olive oil. Reserve ¼ cup of sauce. Place half of remaining sauce along with chicken in a sealable plastic bag and the other half with vegetables in a separate bag. Marinate in refrigerator for 40 minutes.

Preheat grill to medium-high and grease grates. Thread chicken onto skewers, and thread vegetables separately onto additional skewers. Arrange skewers on grill, placing vegetables in direct contact with surface. Flip after 4 to 5 minutes. Grill until chicken and vegetables are cooked through and golden brown, 8 to 10 minutes more. (Vegetables may take a few minutes longer.) Arrange on platter and drizzle with reserved sauce. If desired, Greek yogurt or sour cream is a nice accompaniment. ◊

Chocolate Coconut Zucchini Bread

It happens every year. The mammoth zucchini suddenly appears through the gnarly vines even though you picked several slender and skinny beauties the day before. Not to worry: this chocolate and coconut combo gets its moist texture from plenty of grated zucchini! Cocoa powder makes this bread extra decadent, and coconut oil and toasted coconut flakes not only give it great flavor but also provide healthy fats and a buttery texture. The final product is so tender and flavorful, you'll never guess it has half the oil and sugar of traditional recipes. **MAKES ONE 9X5–INCH LOAF**

2 large eggs, at room temperature

⅓ cup packed brown sugar

⅓ cup honey (or agave nectar)

⅓ cup plus 1 tablespoon unrefined coconut oil, melted

¼ cup nonfat plain yogurt

2 teaspoons vanilla

1⅔ cups all-purpose flour (or 233 grams all-purpose gluten-free flour mix; see pages 9–10)

1 teaspoon baking powder

1 teaspoon baking soda

½ cup unsweetened Dutch-process cocoa powder

½ teaspoon kosher salt

1 teaspoon espresso powder (optional)

1½ cups coarsely shredded zucchini

¼ cup unsweetened coconut flakes

....

Preheat oven to 350 degrees and use parchment paper to create a sling in a 9x5–inch loaf pan. In mixing bowl, whisk together eggs, sugar, honey, coconut oil, yogurt, and vanilla. In a separate large bowl, mix together flour, baking powder, baking soda, cocoa powder, salt, and espresso powder (if using). Add wet ingredients to dry ingredients and stir until just combined and no flour is visible. Fold in zucchini. Pour into parchment-lined loaf pan and smooth batter (which will be thick) to evenly distribute. Top with coconut, gently pressing into batter. Bake for 40 to 45 minutes, until a wooden pick comes out clean. Cool bread in pan on wire rack for 5 minutes, then remove sling and let loaf fully cool. ◇

Decadent Zucchini Brownies with Chocolate Buttercream

These brownies hold a secret that differentiates them from hundreds of zucchini brownie recipes. Here, the green goddess is pureed and disappears into the chocolaty batter as it bakes so even a keen eye won't detect the healthiness packed into this sweet treat. Plus, there's no risk of zucchini shreds finding their way into your teeth, making for an embarrassing smile. Although the espresso powder is optional, I find it creates amazing depth that will make these already decadent brownies completely irresistible. **MAKES ONE 9X13–INCH PAN**

- 2 cups all-purpose flour (or 250 grams all-purpose gluten-free flour mix; see pages 9–10)
- 1 teaspoon baking powder
- ½ teaspoon kosher salt
- 2 teaspoons espresso powder (optional)
- ½ cup unsweetened cocoa powder
- 1 large egg
- ⅓ cup unsalted butter, melted and cooled
- 2 cups skin-on, coarsely chopped zucchini whirled in a blender to make 1 cup of puree
- 1 cup sugar
- 2 teaspoons vanilla

FROSTING

1 cup (2 sticks) unsalted butter, at room temperature

2½–3 cups powdered sugar

1 teaspoon vanilla

4 ounces semisweet or dark chocolate, melted and cooled

....

Preheat oven to 350 degrees. Grease a 9x13–inch pan. In a large bowl, whisk together flour, baking powder, salt, espresso powder (if using), and cocoa powder; set aside. In a separate bowl, whisk together egg, butter, zucchini, sugar, and vanilla. Add liquid mixture to dry ingredients, stirring until smooth. Pour into prepared pan and spread out evenly. Bake for 20 to 25 minutes, until a wooden pick comes out clean or with a few moist crumbs. Let cool completely.

For frosting, use a stand mixer to whip butter on medium-high speed for 5 minutes, stopping once or twice to scrape the bowl. Reduce speed to low and gradually add powdered sugar. Once all of the powdered sugar is incorporated, increase speed and add vanilla, mixing until incorporated. Add melted chocolate and whip at medium-high speed until light and fluffy, about 2 minutes, scraping the bowl as needed to incorporate all of the chocolate. Frost brownies with as thick a layer as you like. Store brownies, covered, in refrigerator for up to 3 days. Let come to room temperature for best flavor. ◇

MAPLE CARDAMOM ZUCCHINI SNACK CAKE

A cake that has vegetables in it must be guilt free, right? Not quite, but we can pretend. With a surplus of zucchini flooding my kitchen it was time to get creative. Instead of a basic zucchini cake, I added ground almonds for texture and my favorite baking spices, cinnamon and cardamom, for an autumnal twist. Fragrant and moist from pure maple syrup, this cake is not overly sweet, which makes it perfect for a midafternoon snack or even a breakfast treat. **MAKES ONE 9X9–INCH FROSTED CAKE**

CAKE

- ½ cup sugar
- ¼ cup plus 1 tablespoon pure maple syrup
- ¼ cup olive oil
- 2 large eggs
- 1½ cups grated zucchini (about 1¼ pounds zucchini)
- 1 teaspoon vanilla
- 1 teaspoon baking soda
- 1 teaspoon baking powder
- 1½ cups all-purpose flour (or 210 grams all-purpose gluten-free flour mix; see pages 9–10)
- ¾ cup almond meal
- pinch kosher salt
- ½ teaspoon cinnamon
- ½ teaspoon cardamom

>>

FROSTING

7	tablespoons unsalted butter, softened
2–2½	cups powdered sugar, sifted
2	teaspoons vanilla
½	teaspoon cinnamon
2–3	tablespoons milk

....

Preheat oven to 325 degrees. Grease and flour a 9x9–inch pan. In a large mixing bowl, whisk together sugar, maple syrup, oil, and eggs, then stir in zucchini. Add vanilla, baking soda, and baking powder to liquid mixture. In a separate bowl, stir together flour, almond meal, salt, cinnamon, and cardamom. Add dry ingredients to wet, stirring to combine. The batter should be slightly thick but easy to pour. Pour batter into prepared pan and bake for 33 to 35 minutes, until a wooden pick comes out clean and the edges are golden brown. Remove from oven and let fully cool in pan set on a wire rack.

For frosting, beat butter for 2 minutes in a stand mixer on medium speed. Reduce mixer to lowest speed and add 1½ cups powdered sugar, mixing until sugar is incorporated. Increase mixer speed to medium, add vanilla, cinnamon, and 2 tablespoons milk, and beat for 2 to 3 minutes. Add ½ cup powdered sugar and beat for 1 minute. If frosting is runny, add more sugar by the tablespoon; if frosting is too thick, add more milk by the tablespoon. Mix until desired consistency. Frost cooled cake and cut into slices. ◊

WINTER
SQUASH

When the cold and snowy midwestern winter drags on and fresh produce is hard to come by, winter squash is my saving grace. Although this book encompasses both summer and winter squash, I'm particularly smitten with the latter. I've never met a vegetable that crosses so many cultural lines or is as versatile in both sweet and savory creations. Humble and comforting, rich and flavorful, unique and intriguing, winter squash boast an inner beauty hidden behind their thick skin. In a weird philosophical way, I think many of us can relate to this in our own personal lives.

Regardless of what kind of winter squash you are buying, it should be heavy for its size. Some varieties like kabocha and buttercup will be covered in harmless rough barnacles, and many will have different color markings. The stem should be dry and corklike, indicating the squash was left on the vine until ripe enough to harvest. The flesh becomes golden and sweet as it matures, soaking up nutrients from the soil and energy from the sun during the long ripening process.

At the market, choose an unblemished squash with a matte rather than glossy skin. A shiny exterior indicates that the fruit was picked too early and won't be as sweet. Try to avoid squash that is bruised or nicked, as the skin is its main source of protection and preservation. After the cold sweeps in, keep an eye out for dark patches on the skin; frostbite shortens shelf life and negatively affects texture. Also, make sure the stem is attached: if it's missing, mold and bacteria are likely to be growing inside.

HARVESTING: Hard-shelled winter squash are ready to pick when the stems are hard and the rind can't be pierced with a thumbnail. It's best to leave them on the vine as long as possible to grow sweeter as the days pass. Before the first heavy frost, cut the stems about an inch above the fruit and let the squash mature in the sun for seven to ten days to harden and cure the skin.

About 90 percent of a winter squash's total weight is water, but it loses much of that moisture as it ages. With age also comes sweetness once the young flesh converts from starch to sugar just as other fruits do when they ripen. Depending on how long ago the farmer picked it, there will be varying levels of sweetness from one squash to the next. Don't be alarmed if your recipe tastes a little different each time you make it.

PRESERVATION: To preserve winter squash, keep them in a cool, well-ventilated, and dark space like a basement. Low humidity is also important, as moisture will cause their insides to rot, which is why you never want to store them whole in the refrigerator. However, you can peel squash, cut it into chunks or halves, then store in the refrigerator for up to four days before using. Freezing is another way to preserve squash if you are without proper long-term storage. Use either of the following methods:

Raw: Peel and cut the squash into chunks of any size; one-inch cubes are good. Spread the pieces in a single layer on a baking sheet and place in the freezer. When squash is completely frozen, transfer to a freezer bag or a glass container with half an inch of headspace to allow for expansion. Frozen chunks may be added directly to stews or soups, but let them thaw if you will be roasting or sautéing.

Cooked: Depending on the size of the squash, cut it in halves, cubes, or slices. Cook until tender by roasting, steaming, or boiling. Remove the skin and mash or puree the squash. When cool, pack the cooked squash into freezer bags and store the bags horizontally for the most efficient use of freezer space. It's also helpful to measure the squash before freezing and label the container with how many cups it contains. This step makes life much easier when it comes time to cook.

NUTRITION: FIVE REASONS TO EAT WINTER SQUASH

No offense to zucchini, but the health benefits of fall-harvest squash far eclipse their summer cousins. They're gold-medal winners when it comes to nutrition and an excellent choice for preparing the body to head into the long midwestern winter.

1. Winter squash's bright orange flesh hints at its most noteworthy health perk: beta carotene. Beta carotene is an antioxidant that protects against unstable free radicals that may cause cancer. Additionally, it can lower the risk of neurological disorders, cardiovascular disease, and diabetes.

2. A heart-healthy choice, winter squash deliver ample doses of dietary fiber, which helps to regulate glucose and cholesterol levels.

3. Winter squash provide significant amounts of potassium, important for bone health, and vitamin B_6, essential for the proper functioning of both the nervous and immune systems.

4. With just a one-cup serving, you'll get nearly half the recommended daily dose of antioxidant-rich vitamin C, and that single cup will only set you back eighty-two calories.

5. Winter squash contain a powerhouse of nutrients known as carotenoids, which have been shown to guard against heart disease and reduce inflammation.

GENERAL METHODS FOR PREPPING WINTER SQUASH

Whether you've cooked with squash a fair amount or you're staring down your first kabocha, these awkward vegetables can be intimidating. Even after all this time, my sweetheart still gets nervous when I've got a big chef's knife in hand, ready to dismantle one. But don't fret: with a few simple tips and the right tools, you'll find squash to be quite manageable.

1. A very sharp chef's knife or cleaver, a good-sized cutting board, and a ceramic peeler will make your squash adventures a lot easier.

2. First, create a flat surface on your squash so that it does not wobble around. Slice off a thin layer from the bottom or sides and knock off the stem.

3. To peel the squash, you have two options. I prefer using a sharp, heavy-duty chef's knife to peel the skin. I find it to be quicker and more efficient. Stand the squash on one of the flat sides you have created, then use the widest part of your knife to shave off the skin. Once you do it a few times, you'll get a feel for taking off wider strips. A Y-shaped ceramic peeler works well, too (much better than a flimsy stainless-steel peeler), because it has ultrasharp blades that won't rust. Note that when working with squash that have ridges or warty bumps, a peeler will not do the job.

4. Cut the squash in half by first inserting the tip of your knife (not the flat middle part, a common mistake) and maintaining steady, downward pressure on the squash. Rock the knife back and forth, guiding it through the rest of the skin.

5. Then, use a melon baller (the best option because it has sharp edges) or spoon to remove the seeds and stringy innards of the squash. A scraping motion with a firm hand will speed up the process. You can even leave the seeds in and scoop them out after roasting if you are short on time.

6. Whether you peel the squash or not, you are now ready to cut the squash into the desired shapes and sizes for your recipe. Make uniform-size pieces to ensure even cooking. Also, remember that squash has a lot of water, so the pieces will shrink as they cook, especially when roasted.

7. If you absolutely can't manage to slice through the squash, bake it whole for 20 minutes at 350 degrees to soften the flesh. From there, proceed with the above steps.

MASTER TECHNIQUES

Roasting

There are many opinions about how to roast squash, but after trying every way possible I've concluded that the best is dry roasting, which results in superior flavor and texture. When I'm using dense, starchy squash like kabocha or buttercup, I roast it cut side down. This helps humidify the flesh and ensure it doesn't dry out. With blander, moister squash like butternut and acorn, I usually roast with cut side up at least part of the time to concentrate the flavor and intensify the natural sugars. Starchier, dense squash like kabocha or red kuri benefit from roasting cut side down to humidify the flesh and ensure it doesn't dry out.

For a puree: Preheat oven to 400 degrees and line a rimmed baking sheet with foil (to make cleanup easier). Rinse the skin of your squash and wipe off any dirt. Cut squash in half and remove seeds using a melon baller, then brush with a light coat of olive oil and sprinkle with salt. Place cut side up or down depending on the squash and roast until squash is very tender and a paring knife can slip through the flesh. The knife should slide out easily and flesh should scoop out like ice cream. If roasting the squash cut side down, turn it face up for about five minutes toward the end of roasting to achieve a slightly deeper flavor. Roasting time can vary from thirty to seventy-five minutes depending on the size and type of squash. Let the squash cool a bit, then scoop flesh into bowl of food processor or blender. Puree on high until smooth, adding a few tablespoons of water if needed.

For roasting as cubes or wedges: Leave the skin on (if edible) or peel it depending on your preference and the intended application. Cut into desired size, then toss or brush with olive oil and salt. Roast on a foil-lined baking sheet in a 400-degree oven until flesh pierces easily with a fork, flipping it halfway through the roasting time to ensure both sides achieve golden edges.

For roasting in halves: If the squash will be halved and stuffed with filling or the flesh used for a mash, roasting it cut side up with the seeds left in results in an even deeper, richer flavor. The seeds' natural oils drip into the flesh as it roasts and provide a nutty flavor. (In fact, Stony Brook WholeHearted Foods, a small New York company, uses seeds from different types of locally farmed squash to make artisan culinary squash oils. They gently roast the seeds, then use a machine to press out the oil. Like high-quality extra-virgin olive oil, each squash oil has a slightly different flavor, ranging from mild umami to the more pronounced taste of roasted peanuts or hazelnuts. You can order it online, which I highly recommend doing.) When the squash is done roasting, the seeds will scoop out easily. You can then use the flesh or fill it with stuffing and bake until warmed through.

Steaming

Steaming winter squash keeps its clean flavor and brilliant color intact. It's a great method for soups, saving you from a lot of chopping when the squash's shape makes it difficult to work with. If you are planning to make a puree from starchy, dense squash like kabocha, steaming works wonders by softening and moistening it. Simply halve the squash or cut into wedges, scoop out the seeds, and place in a steamer basket. Fill a pot with a couple inches of water and bring to a boil, then place the basket above the water level and cover the pot to steam. If the steamed squash is for a savory application, create a natural stock by adding salt, a few slices of onion, and fresh herbs to the boiling water underneath.

Cucurbita Moschata

This subgroup of winter squash includes what I would consider the most recognizable and popular squash, the butternut, as well as a variety of pumpkin that is used commercially and found in cans. Varieties in this species are usually long and oblong with tan rather than orange skin, or round with a peach hue.

BUTTERNUT SQUASH

Butternut squash stole my heart and instigated my love affair with the Cucurbit family. It is one of the most versatile and widely available winter squash because of its resistance to disease. In a pinch you can substitute butternut in pretty much any recipe that calls for squash. Its firm, dense texture makes it ideal for roasting, pureeing, and sautéing. It becomes sweet and nutty when roasted but also has a hint of vegetal flavor that distinguishes it from other varieties.

IDENTIFICATION: Butternut squash is one of the easiest to recognize. Unlike other types whose markings and size can dramatically differ, butternuts always have pale, taupe-colored hard skin and a graceful hourglass figure. Their stems are smooth and grooved. Some have giraffe-like necks and a tinier bulb at the end, while others are squat and short with a fatter bulb. Either way, its shape is ideal for packing into boxes, which is why you can find butternuts at almost any market or grocery store from late August to February.

THE INSIDE SCOOP: A butternut's skin should be smooth, revealing dense, vibrant orange flesh when peeled. Here's a great tip from a local cooking instructor: think about the end product of whatever you're making when picking the shape. For roasting or sautéing the squash in cubes or wedges, choose one that has a long, straight neck with a tinier bulb. It will be easier to peel and cut into uniform pieces because of its length, and it will have fewer seeds. If you're going to puree or mash it, pick one with a larger bulb and don't worry about the neck being straight since you will be roasting the entire thing in its shell and scooping out the flesh anyway. You can substitute butternut squash in almost any recipe that calls for pumpkin or sweet potato, and vice versa. Another alternative: try grating it and using it as a substitute for raw carrots in baked goods or casseroles.

ONE EASY DISH: Roast peeled and cubed squash tossed in olive oil and salt in a 400-degree oven until fork tender. Remove from oven and toss with fried sage and crumbled blue cheese, preferably a creamy version like Shepherd's Way Big Woods Blue. Enjoy it as a side dish or even on toasted baguette slices for a fall bruschetta.

Stuffed Endive Boats with Rosemary-Roasted Squash and Goat Cheese

Keep it simple and delicious with these eye-catching endive boats that can be prepared a day ahead of time with little effort. In this party-friendly appetizer, the endive's sturdy leaf becomes the delivery vehicle—no plates or utensils needed. In the midst of heavy appetizers and sweets during the holidays, this one is a light and refreshing change of pace. **MAKES ABOUT 30 BOATS**

....

3 cups peeled, seeded butternut squash cut into quarter-inch cubes

1 teaspoon kosher salt

¼ teaspoon black pepper

2 tablespoons olive oil

2 sprigs rosemary rubbed with a little olive oil and cut in half

1¼ pounds Belgian endive (about 5 heads)

5 ounces goat cheese

local honey (my favorite is from Ames Farm)

....

Preheat oven to 375 degrees. Toss squash in a bowl with salt, pepper, and olive oil. Place rosemary sprigs on baking sheet and scatter squash on top. Bake for 12 to 14 minutes, stirring once, until fork tender but not falling apart. While squash is roasting, trim bottom of endive heads, then separate leaves. Remove squash from oven and discard rosemary; let cool.

Fill lower half of endive leaves with 2 teaspoons roasted squash (or more, depending on size of leaves) and crumbled goat cheese. Drizzle with honey. Taste and sprinkle with a little more salt if needed. Serve on a large platter, positioned in a circle. ◇

SEARED SQUASH AND BRUSSELS SPROUT SKEWERS WITH GARLIC-THYME AIOLI

Two truths come with this recipe. One, everything is more fun to eat when on a skewer and accompanied by an addicting dipping sauce. And two, you might just end up popping squash and Brussels sprouts like they're potato chips, except they're super healthy! While the veggies are roasting and caramelizing, a robust, semi-homemade garlic-thyme aioli comes together in minutes. And in true Minnesota fashion, they're served on a stick! **SERVES 10–12 AS AN APPETIZER**

AIOLI

- ¼ teaspoon kosher salt
- 1 clove garlic, minced
- ½ cup mayonnaise (I use the type made with olive oil)
- 1 tablespoon water
- 1 teaspoon olive oil
- 1½ tablespoons minced fresh thyme

SKEWERS

- 1 pound Brussels sprouts, outer leaves removed and root end sliced off
- 4 tablespoons olive oil, divided
- 2 tablespoons balsamic vinegar, divided
- 1 teaspoon kosher salt, divided
- 1 medium butternut squash (about 1½ pounds), peeled, seeded, and cut into one-inch cubes

wooden skewers

For the aioli: Place minced garlic on a cutting board and sprinkle with salt. Using the back of a spoon, smear it repeatedly into the cutting board to create a paste. Add mixture to a bowl with remaining ingredients and whisk thoroughly. Cover and set in refrigerator for an hour (and up to a day) before serving so flavors can mingle.

Preheat oven to 400 degrees. Cut Brussels sprouts in half and toss with 2 tablespoons olive oil, 1 tablespoon balsamic vinegar, and ½ teaspoon salt. Place cut side down on a greased baking sheet. Toss cubed squash with remaining 2 tablespoons olive oil, 1 tablespoon balsamic vinegar, and ½ teaspoon salt. Spread onto separate baking sheet, leaving space between the pieces. Put Brussels sprouts on middle rack and squash on lower rack. Roast for 12 to 15 minutes, then check Brussels sprouts, turning over to see if they have a golden-brown sear. When they are seared, remove from oven. Move squash to middle rack, stir, and continue to roast for another 15 minutes, until easily pierced with a fork but not falling apart.

Thread vegetables onto skewers, alternating between squash and Brussels sprouts, piercing sprouts so that the seared half is showing outward for presentation. Arrange on platter with aioli. ◇

Orange Butter–Glazed Brussels Sprouts and Butternut Squash

Every year I wait for the "Jolly Green Giant" Brussels sprouts stalks to appear at the market. For many people they're a "love or hate 'em" kind of vegetable, and coincidentally squash can be the same way. I couldn't resist sautéing the two together in an orange butter glaze to turn skeptics into believers. Bold flavors and textures come from local honey, pecans, and a hefty dose of black pepper, resulting in a side dish that begs for a place on your Thanksgiving table. If you're a carnivore at heart, some crispy, crumbled bacon stirred in at the end is a divine addition. **SERVES 4–5 AS A SIDE DISH**

GLAZE

2 tablespoons butter, melted

2 tablespoons local honey (I like Ames Farm)

1 tablespoon orange zest

3 tablespoons fresh orange juice

½ teaspoon black pepper

2 teaspoons apple cider vinegar

VEGETABLES

2 tablespoons olive oil, divided

1½ pounds butternut squash, peeled, seeded, and cut into quarter-inch cubes (about 3 cups)

kosher salt

1 pound Brussels sprouts, rinsed, trimmed, and halved

½ cup pecans, coarsely chopped

⅓ cup dried cranberries

Stir together glaze ingredients and set aside. In a large skillet, heat 1 tablespoon olive oil over medium heat. Swirl to coat pan, then add squash. Stir the squash pieces so they are coated with oil and sprinkle with ¼ teaspoon salt. Shake pan so squash spreads out in an even layer and let cook, without stirring, so that pieces brown a bit on one side, about 6 to 8 minutes. Stir and spread the pieces out again and let cook, without stirring, until the other side is browned, about 8 minutes. Stir contents and shake pan, cooking until squash pierces easily with a fork but still holds its shape. Remove from heat and pour into a bowl.

In the same pan, heat remaining tablespoon of oil over medium-high heat. When the oil is very hot, place Brussels sprouts cut side down in pan, sprinkling with ½ teaspoon salt. Reduce heat to medium, and sear on one side until nicely browned, about 3 minutes. Turn over Brussels sprouts and cook the other side until browned and tender, 3 to 5 minutes. Some of the leaves that have fallen loose will be dark brown or charred, but don't toss them. They're so good! Reduce heat to low and add squash back to the pan, along with pecans and cranberries. Stir in the glaze to coat all ingredients, then cook for a few minutes, until warmed through. ◊

Minnesota Wild Rice and Butternut Squash Salad with Maple-Balsamic Vinaigrette

I can't tell you how many times I've given out the recipe for this splendid autumn salad that includes some of Minnesota's very best natural ingredients. Warm wild rice not only provides a tender chew and classic nutty flavor but also wilts the spinach. Combined with caramelized squash, then tossed in a simple vinaigrette, this salad is the essence of fall. **SERVES 6 AS A SIDE DISH**

....

SALAD

2½ cups peeled, seeded butternut squash
   cut into quarter-inch cubes

1½ tablespoons olive oil

 sea salt

 black pepper

2½ cups thinly sliced spinach

 ½ cup thinly sliced leeks, white and light green parts

 ½ cup dried cherries (or dried cranberries)

 ¼ cup thinly sliced fresh basil

 3 cups cooked wild rice, warmed

DRESSING

 ¼ cup extra-virgin olive oil

 2 tablespoons pure maple syrup

 2 tablespoons balsamic vinegar

 ½ teaspoon sea salt

 scant ½ teaspoon black pepper

 ½ tablespoon chopped fresh rosemary

 1 clove garlic, minced

....

Preheat oven to 400 degrees. Toss squash with olive oil, salt, and pepper. Spread onto a baking sheet and roast for about 25 minutes, stirring once, until fork tender. In a large bowl, combine spinach, leeks, cherries, and basil. Stir in warm rice and squash so that spinach wilts slightly from the heat. Prepare dressing by pureeing all ingredients with an immersion blender or by vigorously whisking. Stir dressing into salad; taste and adjust salt level if needed. Serve at room temperature. ◊

WHITE BEANS AND BUTTERNUT SQUASH WITH CRISPY CHARD

Between the toasty squash cubes and the crispy chard chips that turn nearly sweet during baking, I'm not sure what's more difficult to stop snacking on while making this dish. This combination of flavors and textures complements each other in a special way. To complete the dish, the squash and chard meet up with creamy white beans simmered with fresh rosemary. Although I prefer cooking them from scratch, there's no shame in using canned beans for a weeknight savior of a meal. **SERVES 3 AS A MAIN DISH, 4 AS A SIDE DISH**

1 cup dried cannellini beans, or 2 (15-ounce) cans cannellini beans, drained and rinsed

2 sprigs fresh rosemary

kosher salt

1 large butternut squash (about 2¼ pounds), peeled, seeded, and cut into 1½–inch cubes

6 tablespoons olive oil, divided

black pepper

6–7 large Swiss chard leaves, roughly chopped (kale would also work)

2 tablespoons balsamic vinegar

1 teaspoon honey

If cooking beans from scratch, soak overnight, covered with 4–5 inches of cold water. Drain beans, add to large pot, and cover with 4 inches cold water. Bring to a boil, then reduce heat to barely a simmer and add the sprigs of rosemary. Cover and cook for 30 minutes, then stir in 1 teaspoon salt. Cook for another 45 to 60 minutes, until beans are tender but not falling apart. Remove from heat, drain, and discard rosemary sprigs. Return beans to pot and set aside. If using canned beans, empty them into a pot.

While beans are cooking (or, if using canned beans, start here), preheat oven to 400 degrees. On baking sheet, toss cubed squash with 2 tablespoons olive oil, ½ teaspoon salt, and pinch of black pepper, then spread out evenly. On a separate baking sheet, toss chard leaves with 1 tablespoon olive oil, ¼ teaspoon salt, and pinch of black pepper. Place both pans in oven and roast chard until crispy, about 10 minutes. Remove from oven and set aside. Continue roasting squash another 20 or so minutes, until cubes pierce easily with a fork. Remove from oven and add squash to pot with beans. Whisk together remaining 3 tablespoons olive oil, balsamic vinegar, honey, ¼ teaspoon salt, and pinch of black pepper. If you did not cook the beans from scratch, finely mince rosemary and add to balsamic mixture, then stir into beans and squash. Taste and adjust seasoning, and add another splash of balsamic if you like. Serve on a large platter or individual plates and top with the crispy chard. ◊

HERB-CRUSTED PORK TENDERLOIN OVER BUTTERNUT-PARSNIP MASH

This comforting winter weeknight meal looks and tastes like it took hours. While the pork is roasting, prepare the squash and parsnips on the stovetop until they become beautifully soft and easy to mash, almost buttery. Stir in a little half-and-half for a luxurious texture without being overindulgent. Although you may be tempted to substitute dried herbs to encrust the pork, fresh are a must as they infuse the pork in a way that dried can't. Additionally, checking the tenderloin's temperature as it roasts, being careful not to overcook, will ensure a juicy, melt-in-your mouth roast. **SERVES 3–4**

TENDERLOIN

1½–2 pound pork tenderloin
(as even as possible in thickness from end to end)

1 tablespoon olive oil

2 cloves garlic, minced

1 teaspoon kosher salt

½ teaspoon black pepper

1 tablespoon minced fresh parsley

1 tablespoon minced fresh thyme

1 tablespoon minced fresh rosemary

MASH

¾ pound parsnips, peeled and cut into one-inch chunks

¾ pound butternut squash, peeled, seeded,
   and cut into one-inch chunks

kosher salt

½ cup half-and-half, at room temperature

⅓ cup freshly grated Parmesan cheese

black pepper

....

Pat pork completely dry with a paper towel. In a small bowl, combine olive oil, garlic, salt, pepper, and herbs. With a firm hand, rub mixture into pork, fully coating all areas. Heat oven to 350 degrees while pork marinates for at least 20 minutes. Then roast pork on a rimmed baking sheet for 20 minutes. Check internal temperature, and continue cooking until the thickest portion reaches 145 degrees (about 40 minutes for a 1½–pound roast), being careful not to overcook. Remove from oven and let rest, covered loosely with foil, for 8 minutes.

While pork is roasting, place parsnips, squash, and a pinch of salt into a pot and cover with water. Bring to a boil, then reduce to a simmer and cook until tender—the tip of a paring knife should pierce without resistance, approximately 20 minutes. Reserve 1 cup cooking water, then drain well. Return vegetables to pot and add half-and-half, cheese, ¼ teaspoon salt, and ¼ teaspoon pepper. Mash to preferred consistency, adding a little cooking water to get the texture you like. Taste and add salt or pepper as needed.

Use a serrated blade to slice pork into half-inch-thick slices and serve over the mash. Drizzle with a touch of olive oil if desired. ◊

BUTTERNUT SQUASH, WHITE BEAN, AND VEGETABLE GRATIN

To say that Twin Cities dwellers are blessed with great access to farmers markets is an understatement. Set along the gorgeous Mississippi River in downtown Minneapolis, the Mill City Farmers Market was founded by Brenda Langton, whole foods educator, chef, and owner of Spoonriver Restaurant. Her main mission was and still is to promote healthy foods, local farmers, and an organic food marketplace. The fruits and vegetables grown by these farmers are some of the most pristine I have ever seen. Sometimes it feels like I'm walking through an art gallery rather than a farmers market. Be sure to make a visit in the fall and pick up the ingredients for this hearty gratin that comes from The Spoonriver Cookbook, *written by Brenda herself as a tribute to her restaurant and the market.* **SERVES 6**

1 medium butternut squash (about 1½ pounds), peeled, seeded, and cut into quarter- to half-inch strips

2 tablespoons olive oil, divided

kosher salt

black pepper

6 cloves garlic, minced

2–3 leeks, white and light green parts, cut in half vertically and rinsed, then thinly sliced (about 2 cups)

1 red bell pepper, cut into thin strips

1½ tablespoons butter

3 cups mushrooms

1 (15-ounce) can white beans, drained and rinsed

4 tomatoes, sliced

¼ cup chopped fresh herbs

½ cup walnuts, coarsely chopped

1 cup shredded Gruyère cheese

....

Preheat oven to 375 degrees. Brush squash with ½ tablespoon olive oil and sprinkle with salt and pepper. Place on a baking sheet and bake 15 minutes or until tender. Remove squash from oven; reduce heat to 350 degrees.

While squash is roasting, heat the remaining 1½ tablespoons olive oil in a skillet over medium heat and add garlic, leeks, and red pepper; cook, stirring, for 5 minutes. Remove vegetables from pan and set aside. Add butter to pan. Melt over medium heat and stir in mushrooms and pinch of salt. Cook for 5 to 6 minutes, until golden brown; set aside.

Layer vegetables in a greased 9x13–inch pan in the following order: squash, mushrooms, white beans, vegetable mix, tomatoes, then herbs. Sprinkle with ½ teaspoon salt and ½ teaspoon pepper, then top with walnuts and cheese. Cover with foil and bake for 30 minutes. Remove foil and bake for an additional 10 minutes, until cheese is bubbling and slightly browned. ◇

VANILLA BEAN BUTTERNUT APPLE CRISP

The fleeting days of summer bring a bit of sadness, but once the scents of cinnamon, nutmeg, and cloves dance down the hall as this dessert bakes, happiness returns. This fruit and vegetable crisp may sound strange, but I assure you tart apples and mellow squash are harmonious partners. The mixture bubbles in a sweet glaze of dark brown sugar, a touch of butter, and speckles of vanilla bean. Use apples that hold their shape when baked, such as Honeycrisp, and cut the two main ingredients into consistently sized cubes so they'll cook evenly. The crumbly streusel lid envelops the mildly sweet filling just right. Serve it à la mode or reheat in the morning and declare it a dessert-for-breakfast kind of day. **MAKES ONE 8x8–INCH PAN**

TOPPING

- ½ cup all-purpose flour (or 70 grams all-purpose gluten-free flour mix; see pages 9–10)
- ½ teaspoon baking soda
- ⅔ cup old-fashioned oats
- ¼ cup almond meal
- ⅓ cup packed dark brown sugar
- ½ teaspoon cinnamon
- ⅛ teaspoon nutmeg
- pinch kosher salt
- 4½ tablespoons unsalted butter, melted

  2 tablespoons unsalted butter

 10 ounces butternut squash, peeled, seeded, and cut
     into quarter-inch cubes (about 2 cups)

  1 pound Honeycrisp or Cortland apples, peeled, cored,
     and cut into half-inch cubes (about 3 cups)

  3 tablespoons sugar

     seeds from 1 vanilla bean cut lengthwise and scraped

  1 tablespoon cornstarch

     whipped cream for serving

....

Preheat oven to 350 degrees. Grease an 8x8–inch pan and set aside. To make topping, stir together dry ingredients (the first 8 listed) in a bowl. Once well mixed, add melted butter and combine with a fork until moist and crumbly.

For the filling, heat a large nonstick skillet over medium heat and melt butter, swirling to cover bottom of pan. Add squash to skillet, stirring to coat. Cook for 4 to 5 minutes over medium heat, then stir in apples, sugar, and vanilla bean seeds. Continue to cook over medium heat for about 8 minutes, stirring occasionally, so squash and apples soften slightly. Add cornstarch, stirring to dissolve, then remove from heat.

Spread squash and apples evenly into prepared pan. Evenly distribute topping mixture, pressing lightly to cover the squash and apples. Bake for 40 to 45 minutes, until top is golden brown and juices are bubbling. Let cool slightly, then serve warm with whipped cream. ◇

ACORN (CUCURBITA PEPO/SUMMER)

When I was a child, *squash* was just a general term to me. I had one vision of what it was and how it could be prepared: a green acorn-looking thing that was cut in half and gutted, then stuffed with brown sugar and butter and set in a pan with a little water to be roasted under a foil covering. Turns out this might just be one of the worst ways to cook an acorn squash, resulting in a watery, flavorless dish that had me believing I hated all squash. Sound familiar? Although acorn is still not my favorite, I've found new ways of cooking with it that have changed my outlook.

IDENTIFICATION: When I started researching squash on a deeper level, I was quite surprised to find out that the acorn is actually part of the Cucurbita pepo, meaning it is a summer squash. Curing the squash hardens the shell and reduces the moisture a bit, but these squash in the pepo family do not store quite as long as you may presume. Usually weighing one to two pounds, acorns are a nice size for two people and are quite glamorous looking with their edible forest-green covering. On the down side, their flesh is highly fibrous and the flavor can be bland and inconsistent. I lean toward their hybrid cousins, Carnival and Heart of Gold varieties, which are a touch sweeter and less fibrous. They are similar in shape and size, so they work just as well for stuffing and a one- or two-person meal. If the skin of the acorn is shiny and completely dark green, that means it's not quite ripe. Pick one that is somewhat dull and has a splash of orange, which signals that it rested in the fields until it was ready to harvest. If you cut it open and it's dark orange, you've got a good squash. If it's light yellow, it won't be as sweet.

THE INSIDE SCOOP: So how did I come to like this squash? Well, I discovered that despite its slightly mellow flavor, it can be combined with other robust foods to make a great meal, and baking surely concentrates its flavor. The skin is edible, but with a little work the squash can be peeled and cubed for meals like risotto, if you choose. Traditionally it is stuffed with grains and protein or roasted with simple seasonings, but I also found that it works well when grated into desserts for moistness. You'll even find a recipe for slicing acorns into wedges for grilling, which has become a fun fall tradition for me.

ONE EASY DISH: Preheat oven to 350 degrees. Halve squash crosswise and remove seeds. Rub cut sides and cavities of squash with softened butter; season with salt and pepper. Slice 2 cloves of garlic and distribute into each half along with fresh thyme and rosemary. Fill each cavity about halfway with cream. Set squash halves on a sheet pan and roast until tender, about 40 minutes. Remove from oven, top with a little more cream and some Gruyère cheese, then return to oven for 10 minutes, until cheese is browned.

Golden Curried Squash Hummus

Over the last couple of years, hummus has been popping up at parties like the classic French onion dip of the eighties. You have probably picked some up on your way out of Trader Joe's with a bottle of two-buck chuck in hand, but it's so simple to make on your own and far tastier. Hummus, a Middle Eastern staple for hundreds of years, is made from pureed chickpeas (garbanzo beans), tahini, and a squeeze of lemon for tart balance. I've created my own spin on the traditional, adding roasted acorn squash, curry powder, and lime juice instead of lemon. Smooth and savory, the warming flavors unravel in layers. It's one of my favorite ways to use up leftover roasted squash. **SERVES 4–6 AS AN APPETIZER**

¾ teaspoon kosher salt

2 cloves garlic

1 (15-ounce) can chickpeas (garbanzo beans), drained and rinsed

¾ cup roasted acorn squash (see master technique, page 75)

3 tablespoons tahini (sesame seed paste)

1 tablespoon olive oil, plus more for garnish

2 tablespoons fresh lime juice

3 tablespoons water, plus up to 3 tablespoons more if needed

3 teaspoons high-quality curry powder

½ teaspoon ground cumin

minced cilantro for garnish

pita bread, crackers, tortilla chips, or veggies for serving

Add salt and garlic to bowl of food processor with blade running (the salt helps keep the garlic from sticking to the blade). Scrape down sides of bowl, and add in chickpeas, squash, tahini, olive oil, lime juice, and water. Process until smooth, adding more water a tablespoon at a time if needed. Add in curry powder and cumin. Process for another 1½ minutes, until completely smooth and slightly warm. Taste and adjust salt if needed. Garnish with a drizzle of olive oil and fresh minced cilantro. Serve with pita bread, crackers, tortilla chips, or veggies. Can be made a day ahead of time. ◇

GRILLED ACORN SQUASH WITH OLIVE TAPENADE

In my opinion, fall is the best time of year to grill. The mild weather and cool nights make standing over the flames quite enjoyable. If you've never grilled squash, you're going to love the result—nutty and luscious wedges with a crisp edge and fluffy inside. Acorn squash's delicate sweetness is a wonderful platform for the big flavor of olives, garlic, and salty capers found in tapenade. In the depths of winter when your grill is hidden under a gigantic blanket of snow, use a grill pan or even a panini press for the same effect.

SERVES 2

1 small acorn squash, halved and seeded

3 tablespoons olive oil, divided

¼ teaspoon kosher salt

balsamic vinegar

olive tapenade (found in condiment section or deli)

Cut squash halves crosswise into half-inch-wide slices. Brush with 1 tablespoon olive oil, completely coating squash, including the skin. Toss with salt. Heat grill (or grill pan) over medium heat until hot. Grill squash, covered, in batches if necessary, flipping occasionally. When you flip the squash, brush it with a little more olive oil. If will take 15 to 20 minutes for the squash to become tender. At that point, remove from heat and brush lightly with balsamic vinegar. Arrange on a platter and spread olive tapenade across the middle of the wedges. ◇

Caramelized Onion and Acorn Squash Soup with Toasted Pecans

Caramelized onions are a delicacy made from patience, one of those "good things come to those who wait" kinds of things. Cooked low and slow, the onions become intensely rich with a complex sweetness and gorgeous caramel color. While the onions undergo their transformation, the squash is roasted, and the two pureed together create a satisfying winter soup, full of depth. Enjoy with a thick slice of bread and a simple salad for a comforting, meatless meal. **SERVES 4**

1 small to medium acorn squash (about 1½ pounds), halved and seeded

1 tablespoon olive oil

1 tablespoon butter

2 medium yellow or white onions (about 1 pound), halved and thinly sliced into half moons

kosher salt

2 cups vegetable stock (or chicken stock), divided

black pepper

¾ cup buttermilk (or whole milk)

¼ cup pecans, toasted and coarsely chopped

Preheat oven to 400 degrees. Brush squash with olive oil, then roast cut side up for about 40 minutes or until flesh pierces easily with a fork. Scoop out flesh and set aside.

While squash is roasting, heat a wide, thick-bottomed stainless-steel skillet over medium heat and add butter, swirling to coat the bottom. Throw in onion slices, scattering them evenly over bottom of pan. Let cook 5 minutes *without stirring* to achieve an initial browning, which will continue to infuse the onions with deep, complex flavors throughout the process. Stir and spread out again, watching as onions begin to "sweat" and soften as water exits the cells. After about 10 minutes, or when onions are soft and most of the moisture is gone, add a big pinch of salt and stir. Reduce heat to medium low and continue to cook for 30 minutes, stirring often enough that they don't burn but not so much that they won't brown. When the onions are a uniform brown color they are finished.

Stir in 1 cup of broth, scraping the bottom of the skillet to get all of the bits and flavor from the onions. Transfer onions and broth to a blender and blend on medium speed for 1 minute. Stop blender and add in half of the squash flesh, the remaining cup of broth, ¼ teaspoon pepper, and ¼ teaspoon salt. Blend at medium speed for another 45 seconds. Stop blender and add in remaining squash and buttermilk. Puree on medium high for 1 to 1½ minutes, until creamy and smooth. Taste and add more salt or pepper if needed; for thinner soup, add more broth. Pour into bowls and top each with a scant tablespoon of chopped pecans. ◇

MOROCCAN LAMB AND QUINOA–STUFFED ACORN SQUASH

Stuffed acorn squash can be fairly boring, but pair it with the flavors of Morocco and your taste buds will dance. The squash is first roasted without the filling so it becomes caramelized and slightly sweet. Meanwhile, ground lamb is sautéed with aromatic spices and combined with beautiful red quinoa, golden raisins, and fresh orange zest. This multicultural mix is spooned into the warm squash halves and topped with crunchy pistachios, resulting in a unique twist on the ordinary. **SERVES 4**

2 small acorn (or Carnival) squash, halved and seeded

olive oil

kosher salt

1¾ cups water

1 cup red quinoa (or white quinoa), rinsed

½ cup golden raisins

½ pound ground lamb (or beef or turkey)

½ teaspoon cinnamon

½ teaspoon cumin

¼ teaspoon paprika

¼ teaspoon black pepper

½ cup leeks, white and green parts, cut in half vertically and rinsed, then thinly sliced crosswise

2 cloves garlic, minced

zest of 1 medium orange

¼ cup fresh orange juice

3 tablespoons minced fresh parsley

toasted pistachios, chopped (optional)

Preheat oven to 400 degrees. Rub squash with a bit of olive oil and salt. Place cut side down on a rimmed baking sheet and roast about 25 minutes. Flip squash and continue baking, cut side up, until you can easily poke a knife through the flesh at its thickest part (about 10 to 20 minutes longer, depending on size). Remove from oven.

While squash is cooking, add water, ¾ teaspoon salt, and quinoa to a pot. Bring to a boil, then reduce to a light simmer and cook, covered, for about 13 minutes, until the little ringlets start to come off of the grains and all or most liquid is absorbed. (Drain excess liquid if needed.) Quinoa should be tender but not mushy. Remove from heat, stir in raisins, and cover for 5 minutes, then fluff with a fork.

Heat large skillet over medium heat. Add lamb, ¾ teaspoon salt, cinnamon, cumin, paprika, and pepper. Cook until browned and no pink remains, about 5 to 7 minutes. Using a slotted spoon, transfer lamb to a paper towel–lined plate, leaving grease in the pan. Return pan to medium heat and stir in leeks and garlic. Cook about 5 minutes, until softened, then remove from heat.

Add lamb, quinoa, orange zest, juice, and parsley to pan with leeks. Stir to fully incorporate. Taste and adjust salt if needed. Fill each squash cavity with the mixture and place back on baking sheet. Cover with foil and return to oven for 6 to 8 minutes to warm through. Remove from oven and top with pistachios (if using). ◇

WEEKNIGHT SPINACH AND ARTICHOKE–STUFFED SQUASH

In this recipe, a healthy riff on the classic spinach and artichoke dip appetizer is nestled into Carnival or Sweet Dumpling squash to make a simple meal for two. With their small size, these squash are just the right vehicle for a gooey, garlicky filling that's topped with Parmesan cheese and toasted breadcrumbs. Take note that the garlic is sliced instead of minced, making it less potent so as to not overpower the squash. **SERVES 4**

2 Carnival squash or Sweet Dumpling squash (about 3½–4 inches in diameter), halved and seeded

½ tablespoon olive oil

1 clove garlic, thinly sliced

6 cups loosely packed spinach (about 2½ ounces), coarsely chopped

¼ teaspoon black pepper

kosher salt

3 tablespoons water

1 (7.5-ounce) jar marinated artichokes, drained and chopped

⅓ cup plus 1 tablespoon plain Greek yogurt

¼ cup grated Parmesan cheese, divided

3 tablespoons breadcrumbs (or gluten-free breadcrumbs)

Preheat oven to 400 degrees. Place squash on a rimmed baking sheet cut side down. Roast for about 35 to 40 minutes, until fork easily pierces flesh. While squash is roasting, heat olive oil in skillet over medium heat. Add garlic and cook, stirring, for 1 minute, until fragrant. Add in spinach, pepper, pinch of salt, and water. Cook, stirring, for a few minutes, until spinach wilts. Add in chopped artichokes and mix together, heating through. (If you think you will need more filling for the squash cavity, add a little more spinach and cook to wilt.) Remove from heat and stir in yogurt and half of Parmesan. Taste and add salt if needed.

When squash is done roasting, stuff cavities evenly. Top with remaining cheese and the breadcrumbs. Return to oven for 7 to 10 minutes, until cheese is melted and breadcrumbs lightly browned. ✧

"You'd Think It Was Carrot" Winter Squash and Coconut Cake

For my mom's birthday, I just had to surprise her with a twisted rendition on her absolute favorite dessert—an ultramoist, classic carrot cake with glorious amounts of fluffy cream cheese frosting. Beaming with trickery and excitement about the delicious result, I revealed the magical squash component as she finished her last bite. Instead of carrots, the secret ingredient here is grated acorn squash, which is folded into the batter with unsweetened coconut just before baking, resulting in a springy and tender cake. I didn't want the autumnal spices to be overshadowed by a thick layer of cream cheese, so I aimed for flavor in the cake itself and went light on the frosting, which I think you'll appreciate. This recipe is dedicated to you, Mom.

To prepare squash: Cut in half and peel (see general method, page 72). Remove seeds, then cut into large chunks and use box grater or food processor with shredding disk to grate. **MAKES ONE 8-INCH DOUBLE LAYER CAKE**

....

DRY INGREDIENTS

2 cups all-purpose flour (or 255 grams all-purpose gluten-free flour mix; see pages 9–10)

½ cup almond meal (50 grams)

1½ teaspoons baking powder

1 teaspoon baking soda

½ teaspoon kosher salt

1 teaspoon cinnamon

1 teaspoon ground ginger

½ teaspoon ground cardamom

WET INGREDIENTS

½ cup melted extra-virgin coconut oil, cooled

¾ cup sugar

¾ cup lightly packed brown sugar

⅓ cup Greek yogurt

1½ teaspoons vanilla

3 large eggs

1½ cups coarsely grated acorn squash (see head note)

½ cup unsweetened coconut

FROSTING

1 (8-ounce) package cream cheese, chilled

5 tablespoons unsalted butter, softened

2 teaspoons vanilla

2½ cups sifted powdered sugar

¼–½ cup unsweetened coconut, toasted, for garnish

....

Preheat oven to 350 degrees. Coat bottoms and sides of 2 (8-inch) cake pans with nonstick spray. In a mixing bowl, stir together dry ingredients. In a separate bowl, using a stand or hand mixer, beat the oil and sugars together on medium speed for 1½ minutes. Add yogurt, vanilla, and eggs and beat for an additional minute on medium speed. With mixer on medium speed, gradually add in dry ingredients, mixing until fully combined. Stir in squash and coconut.

Divide batter between prepared pans and lightly tap on counter to release any air bubbles. Bake for about 30 minutes, until lightly browned and a wooden pick comes out clean. Let cool for 8 minutes in pan, then invert both cakes onto a cooling rack and let cool completely.

> >

For frosting, beat cold cream cheese with butter and vanilla until combined, about 30 seconds. With mixer on low speed, gradually add 2 cups powdered sugar. Continue to add up to another ½ cup of powdered sugar until you reach desired consistency and sweetness. Place one of the cake layers upside down on serving plate and spread top with about 1 cup frosting. Cover with remaining cake layer and spread top with remaining frosting. Garnish with toasted coconut.

Store this cake in the refrigerator so the cream cheese frosting doesn't lose stability, for up to 3 days. ◇

Winter Squash and Coconut Cake

SPAGHETTI (*CUCURBITA PEPO/SUMMER*)

Although spaghetti squash doesn't appear in midwestern markets until late August, it is actually a summer squash, part of the Cucurbita pepo family like acorn squash. With an inside that turns into delicate golden strands once roasted, this squash is in a league of its own. Many people praise it as a low-calorie stand-in for pasta, and although it does resemble angel hair pasta, its texture and taste are completely different. I find most who have this vision are disappointed after their first experience. To truly appreciate its brilliance, think of it as a rock star squash that juliennes itself.

IDENTIFICATION: Easily identifiable with a pale yellow color and oblong shape similar to a watermelon, spaghetti squash can range anywhere from two to six pounds. As with other summer squash, bigger is not always better. With an increase in size they become bland, with more seeds and tougher skin. Look for one that is more yellow than white, a sign it was harvested when ripe. Since it is a summer squash, it has a shortened storage time, about one to two months at most.

THE INSIDE SCOOP: My shift in attitude about spaghetti squash was a result of finally learning that the reason it was often flavorless and mushy was due to overcooking. Most recipes instruct you to "roast for forty-five minutes until easily pierced with a fork," like other varieties of squash, but by that time the flesh is usually overcooked and won't separate into strands. Instead, roast it cut side down for about twenty-five minutes, then poke at the flesh to see if it will separate into strands. If not, continue roasting, checking every five minutes until it separates, and you'll end up with al dente julienned squash. With a flavor that's sweeter and more vegetal than pasta, it's a good companion to spices, garlic, and acidic vegetables like tomatoes. Blended into a puree, spaghetti squash also makes a lovely soup.

To make the strands: Roast twenty to thirty minutes, until strands separate when scraped with a fork and still have a firm texture. If you scrape from side to side instead of the length of the squash, you will get longer noodles. If some of the strands clump or gather together, simply separate them using your hands.

ONE EASY DISH: Roast halved and seeded spaghetti squash cut side down in a 350-degree oven for 25 to 30 minutes, until strands separate easily when scraped with a fork. Remove strands from cooked halves. Sauté 2 cloves minced garlic in 2 tablespoons olive oil until fragrant, then stir in squash, lots of fresh herbs (like rosemary and parsley), salt, and freshly grated Parmesan.

Fresh Herb and Gruyère Spaghetti Squash Sauté

There's nothing better than a dish that's pure, uncluttered, and utterly delish. Given spaghetti squash's mild sweetness and gorgeously thin strands, I find I even prefer it to true pasta. Fresh herbs and garlic join the delicate squash in a fantastically crunchy swirl of savory pine nuts and creamy Gruyère. Ready in less than an hour, this last-minute side dish is one I can always count on. Pair it with a glass of citrusy Sauvignon Blanc and great conversation for simple happiness. **SERVES 4 AS A SIDE DISH**

1 medium spaghetti squash (about 2½ pounds), halved and seeded

olive oil

kosher salt

2 cloves garlic, minced

2 teaspoons white wine vinegar

¼ cup minced fresh parsley

2 tablespoons minced fresh basil

¾ cup shredded Gruyère cheese

½ cup pine nuts, toasted

black pepper

Preheat oven to 375 degrees. Rub squash with a bit of olive oil and sprinkle with salt. Place cut side down on a rimmed baking sheet and roast for about 25 minutes, until fork tender. Let cool about 10 minutes, then scrape the insides with a fork to pull the strands away from the skin.

In a large skillet, heat 2½ tablespoons olive oil over medium heat. Add garlic and cook for about 1½ minutes, until fragrant. Stir in spaghetti squash, vinegar, herbs, and ¼ teaspoon salt. Cook for about 2 minutes to heat through. Remove from heat and stir in Gruyère cheese, then top with pine nuts. Taste and add salt or pepper if needed. ◇

Savory Spaghetti Squash Cakes with Poached Eggs and Harissa

A cross between a fritter and a thin pancake, these savory spaghetti squash cakes have become one of my favorite things to serve at a champagne brunch. The squash is infused with garlic as it roasts, then mixed with coriander and fresh chives. As the cakes cook, the insides stay moist and the edges crisp up, their crunchiness contrasting with the pillowy poached eggs. Harissa is the African equivalent to sriracha, a smoky red chili sauce traditionally served with eggs, hence its inclusion here. There are a few components to the recipe, but you can make the cakes a day ahead, then crisp them in a hot oven before serving. **SERVES 4**

1 medium spaghetti squash (about 3 pounds), halved and seeded

olive oil

kosher salt

black pepper

2 cloves garlic, peeled

2 tablespoons minced fresh chives

1 large egg, lightly beaten, plus 4 large eggs

¾ cup all-purpose flour (or 105 grams all-purpose gluten-free flour mix; see pages 9–10)

½ teaspoon ground coriander

⅓ cup grated Parmesan cheese

canola oil for frying

1 teaspoon vinegar

1 cup lightly packed spinach

minced cilantro

store-bought harissa (found in the condiment section)

Preheat oven to 375 degrees. Rub squash with a little olive oil and sprinkle with salt and pepper. Rub garlic cloves with a little olive oil and place on baking sheet, then cover each with a squash half, cut side down. Roast squash for 25 to 30 minutes, until strands pull away from the skin and are al dente. Remove from oven and let cool slightly, setting aside softened garlic. Using a fork, scrape out squash flesh and measure 3 cups of squash, saving remaining flesh for another recipe.

Squeeze liquid out of the squash by placing strands in the middle of a large towel, rolling it up, and wringing it out. Place squash in a large bowl and toss with chives. Mash the softened garlic with a fork, then whisk it with the beaten egg. Add egg mixture, flour, coriander, Parmesan, and ¾ teaspoon salt to squash, stirring to combine and then mixing with your hands. The mixture should hold together but still be a little wet and sticky. If it's too wet, mix in 1 tablespoon flour at a time until it holds together.

Heat a large skillet over medium-high heat and add canola oil to cover the surface to a depth of about ¼ inch. When hot, drop ¼-cup portions of batter in the pan and flatten with the back of the measuring cup to make round cakes. Cook about 4 to 5 minutes, until golden on one side, then flip and repeat. Alternatively, bake cakes on a greased baking sheet in a 375-degree oven for approximately 8 minutes on each side.

Bring a medium saucepan of water to barely a boil and add vinegar. Crack one egg into a small dish and, working close to the water, slide it in. Quickly do the same with up to 2 more eggs. As you slide the eggs into the water, adjust the temperature to maintain a simmer. Set timer for 4 minutes. After a minute or so, gently slip a spatula under each egg to make sure it is not sticking to the bottom of the pan. When the timer goes off, remove eggs with a slotted spoon and carefully blot with paper towels to remove water. Repeat with any remaining eggs.

To serve, cover each cake with a few leaves of spinach and cilantro, then slide an egg on top with a spoonful of harissa. Garnish with more cilantro and a pinch of salt. ◇

MEXICAN SPAGHETTI SQUASH BOWLS WITH SMASHED AVOCADO

Who needs a deep-fried taco shell when you can pile all your favorite Mexican fixin's onto a tender bed of spaghetti squash with zero guilt? Roast the squash, scoop out the strands, and build the bowl to your liking. Black beans, zesty spices, and avocado are my essentials. Normally I use a spicy salsa, but sometimes I switch it up with a fruit version, like mango chipotle. And for extra protein, I often add a poached egg. The buttery yolk coats the spaghetti strands beautifully. All in all, it's a pretty ridiculous pile of healthy goodness if I do say so myself. **SERVES 2–3**

1 small spaghetti squash (about 2 pounds), halved and seeded

1½ tablespoons olive oil

1 clove garlic, minced

¼ cup minced green bell pepper

½ teaspoon kosher salt

1½ teaspoons chili powder

1 teaspoon cumin

1 cup canned black beans, drained and rinsed

1 avocado, flesh removed and mashed with ¼ teaspoon kosher salt

spicy salsa

cilantro

1 lime

Preheat oven to 400 degrees. Place squash cut side down on baking sheet. Roast for 20 to 25 minutes, until squash pierces easily with a paring knife. Allow squash to cool about 3 to 4 minutes. Using a sturdy fork, scrape the insides to pull strands away from the skin. You will need about 3½ cups of strands.

Heat olive oil in a skillet over medium heat. Stir in garlic and green pepper. Cook, stirring, for 3 to 4 minutes, until softened, then stir in spaghetti squash. Add salt, chili powder, and cumin, stirring to coat. Add in black beans, and cook for 5 to 6 minutes.

Place desired amount of squash and black bean mixture into 2 to 3 serving bowls. Divide mashed avocado and salsa between bowls. Sprinkle with fresh cilantro and a hefty squeeze of lime juice. ◇

Spaghetti Squash Lasagna with Butter-Roasted Tomato Sauce

Whether you're trying to watch your carb intake or just looking for a way to satisfy an Italian craving, I guarantee you'll enjoy this healthier take on lasagna. Thin strands of spaghetti squash are layered with ricotta, mozzarella, and my favorite homemade tomato sauce. Instead of simmering the sauce on the stove, roast the tomatoes with butter and a good amount of veggies for deep flavors at the same time as the squash, killing two birds with one stone. The most important step of this recipe involves squeezing as much water out of the roasted squash as you can so that the dish is not diluted with liquid. I like to prepare the sauce and squash the day before, then assemble and bake the next day. **SERVES 5–6**

SAUCE

- 1 (15-ounce) can diced tomatoes with basil
- 1 (15-ounce) can fire-roasted crushed tomatoes
- 1½–2 cups thinly sliced mushrooms (about 8 ounces)
- 1 cup chopped onions
- 3 cloves garlic, thinly sliced
- 2 tablespoons thinly sliced fresh basil
- 1 tablespoon balsamic vinegar
- ½ teaspoon kosher salt
- ¼ teaspoon black pepper
- 2½ tablespoons butter, cut into cubes

LASAGNA

1 large spaghetti squash (about 3½ pounds), halved and seeded

olive oil

kosher salt

¼ cup thinly sliced fresh basil

1 cup full-fat ricotta cheese

1 large egg, lightly beaten

black pepper

3 cups shredded mozzarella, divided

....

Preheat oven to 375 degrees. Stir together sauce ingredients in a baking pan. Cover pan with foil. Brush squash with a thin layer of olive oil and sprinkle with a pinch of salt, then place cut side down on a baking sheet. Place both pans in the oven. After 30 minutes, remove foil from the sauce and stir. Continue roasting both pans, uncovered, for another 15 to 20 minutes, until a fork can easily pull away the squash strands and they are al dente.

Remove both pans from oven. Turn spaghetti squash cut side up and let cool until safe to touch. Use a sturdy fork to remove strands by scraping the flesh of the squash. Here's the important part: put strands into a large kitchen towel, roll up as you would a burrito, and squeeze out as much water as you can from the strands. Place drained strands into a bowl and toss with basil and ¼ teaspoon salt.

In a 7x10–inch or other deep casserole dish, spread 1¼ cups of sauce on the bottom to cover. Cover sauce evenly with half of the squash strands, pressing gently to flatten. In a separate bowl, whisk together ricotta, egg, ¼ teaspoon salt, and ¼ teaspoon pepper. Stir in 1 cup mozzarella cheese, then spread onto spaghetti squash layer. Spread 2 cups of sauce on top of ricotta, followed by the remaining spaghetti squash. Evenly cover the squash with 2 cups mozzarella. Cover with foil and bake in a 375-degree oven for 30 minutes, then remove foil and bake for another 10 to 15 minutes, until lasagna is bubbly and cheese has melted. Remove from oven and let sit for 8 minutes, then use serrated knife to cut into slices. Will keep in refrigerator for 4 days. ◇

DELICATA (CUCURBITA PEPO/*SUMMER*)

Thankfully, my significant other has forgiven me for waxing poetically about the second love of my life, delicata squash. When roasted it becomes caramelized and sweet as candy, and to tell you the truth I craved it more than chocolate as I wrote this book. It's the least labor-intensive squash of them all: roasting literally takes no more time than slice-and-bake cookies (in a much healthier form!). Although fairly easy to find, delicata disappear a little earlier in the fall than butternut or acorn, so be sure to savor them while you can. I'm certain they will become one of your "main squeezes," too.

IDENTIFICATION: Oblong in shape, a delicata is yellow with green (indicating peak maturity) and orange vertical stripes. Its flesh is sunshine yellow with a flavor that mimics sweet potatoes and hazelnuts. When buying, pick ones with smooth, unblemished skin that feel firm, especially near the stem ends. They'll keep for several weeks in a cool, dark place. The small, globe-shaped Sweet Dumpling squash is related to the delicata, evidenced by the same green and yellow ribbed markings as well as the dry, starchy flesh with a sweet potato flavor. Both are an ideal squash when cooking for one or two.

THE INSIDE SCOOP: The puree of delicata is a gorgeous, golden straw color with a honeylike sweetness. Along with kabocha, it's my preferred choice for desserts like pies, puddings, and quick breads. On the savory side, I like a simple preparation to appreciate the flavor and texture of delicata, which holds its shape beautifully. The skin is edible, so no peeling is required. I love making half-moon slices, popping them in the oven for a quick roast (fifteen to twenty minutes to tenderness), then tossing them on top of salad or breakfast hash. Beyond roasting in slices, you can also stuff the squash with a combination of just about anything, like one of my standbys: brown rice and sautéed greens with a sprinkling of Fontina cheese.

ONE EASY DISH: Cut delicata in half lengthwise and rub flesh with olive oil and a bit of salt. Roast cut side up at 375 degrees for 20 to 25 minutes, until flesh pierces easily with a fork. Scoop out seeds, then scoop out the flesh and mash with fresh ricotta and flaky sea salt. Spread onto baguette slices and top with chopped pistachios and a drizzle of olive oil.

SWEET AND SALTY ROASTED SQUASH SEEDS

I'm always looking for ways to use all the parts of fruits or vegetables instead of tossing them out. For instance, did you know that squash skin adds significant depth to a homemade vegetable stock? These roasted squash seeds are an excellent plant-based source of fiber and protein, plus they satisfy my snack craving when I just can't decide between sweet and savory. The recipe calls for boiling the seeds before letting them dry. This may seem like extra work, but since the insides cook much faster than the shell, it keeps them from burning. I like to use delicata because they yield a fair amount of seeds, but kabocha, butternut, and acorn work well, too. **MAKES 2 CUPS**

>>

....

2 cups squash seeds, pulp removed, seeds thoroughly rinsed

1 tablespoon butter, melted

1 teaspoon vanilla

1 teaspoon kosher salt

2 tablespoons brown sugar

¼ teaspoon cinnamon

pinch black pepper

....

Add squash seeds to a pot of water and bring to a boil. Reduce to a simmer and cook for 10 minutes. Drain, then rub seeds with a towel to remove excess water and then spread onto a towel to dry for an hour.

Preheat oven to 325 degrees. In a large mixing bowl, stir together the dried seeds and butter, then the remaining ingredients. Spread onto a parchment paper–lined baking sheet and bake for 10 minutes, then stir. Bake for another 5 to 10 minutes so that seeds caramelize, but keep an eye on them because they can turn from brown to black quite quickly. Remove from oven and allow to cool on the baking sheet. Store in an airtight container for up to 3 days. ◇

WARM DELICATA AND KALE JEWEL SALAD

Over the last few years, kale has definitely become the popular kid among nutrient-dense greens. Massaging raw kale reduces the bitterness and softens the leaves, but in the winter I like to make this warm salad and let the heat do that job. This colorful salad with roasted delicata squash and ruby-red pomegranate seeds feels holiday-esque and adds welcome color to any plate. The delicata squash caramelizes in the oven, becoming extraordinarily sweet and tender. With a sprinkle of pomegranate seeds and a light mustard dressing, it's a lovely complement to roasted chicken or braised short ribs.

SERVES 4 AS A SIDE DISH

....

  1 large delicata squash, halved, seeded, and cut into half-inch-thick half moons

2½ tablespoons olive oil, divided

    kosher salt

  2 tablespoons coarse-ground mustard

  1 tablespoon red wine vinegar

  2 tablespoons honey

 ¼ teaspoon black pepper

  1 large bunch kale, stems removed, leaves coarsely chopped

  3 tablespoons water

 ½ cup pomegranate seeds

....

Preheat oven to 400 degrees. Coat squash with 1 tablespoon olive oil and a light sprinkling of salt, and spread onto a parchment paper–lined baking sheet. Bake until just tender, 15 to 18 minutes.

Meanwhile, in a small bowl, mix together remaining 1½ tablespoons olive oil, mustard, red wine vinegar, honey, pepper, and ¼ teaspoon salt. Place kale and water in a large nonstick skillet over medium heat. Stir to coat kale with water and let cook for 3 minutes, stirring to slightly massage kale and reduce its toughness. Cover and cook for an additional 8 minutes, then check to see if it is softened to your liking. Cook a few more minutes if still tough. Remove from heat when wilted, and stir in dressing. Add squash to kale and gently stir. Taste and adjust seasoning as needed, top with pomegranate seeds, and serve warm. Will keep in refrigerator for 3 days. ◇

Miso Sesame Delicata Squash

Here's an Asian-inspired recipe that's quick and easy to make, inspired by an irresistible miso dressing served at Birchwood Cafe in Minneapolis. You can bypass peeling the beautiful and edible striped delicata skin and wait for the crescent-shaped slices to caramelize while they roast, highlighting the sweet, hazelnut-flavored flesh. Balanced by the salty complexity of miso (fermented soybean paste) and sesame seed oil, this simple combination works brilliantly. The arugula's peppery bite is a key flavor profile in this dish, so be sure to seek out this tender green. **SERVES 3–4 AS A SIDE DISH**

1 large delicata squash (about 1¼ pounds), halved, seeded, and cut into half-inch-thick half moons

1 tablespoon olive oil

3½ teaspoons sesame oil, divided

1 clove garlic, smashed

2 tablespoons white miso (found in the refrigerator section of most grocery stores and always at Asian markets)

3 tablespoons fresh lime juice, divided

¼ cup water

kosher salt

1½ cups arugula (or spinach)

¼ cup toasted pepita seeds

Preheat oven to 400 degrees. Toss squash with olive oil and spread on a rimmed baking sheet so that slices are not touching. Bake for about 25 minutes or until tender, flipping halfway through roasting.

Meanwhile, heat 2 teaspoons sesame oil in a small saucepan over medium-low heat. Add smashed garlic and gently cook for about 1 minute, until garlic is fragrant and has infused the oil. Remove and discard clove, then add miso, 2 tablespoons lime juice, and water. Stir until smooth and the dressing is warm. Season to taste with salt.

Toss arugula with remaining 1½ teaspoons sesame oil and 1 tablespoon lime juice, then spread onto plate or divide among 4 plates. Arrange squash on top of arugula, and drizzle with the warm miso dressing. Top with toasted pepitas. ◇

DELICATA, SPINACH, AND CHICKPEA RED CURRY

Stuck in a dinnertime rut? This curry is a wholesome one-pot meal that comes together in less than an hour. The slender green-and-yellow-striped delicata is braised in this Southeast Asian–inspired recipe, browned first with aromatic Thai curry paste, then simmered in coconut milk. Briefly frying the spices and lemongrass in coconut oil makes the flavors intense and robust. The sweet squash, the nutty chickpeas, and the heavy hit of lemongrass offer a respite from the heat. Lemongrass is sold fresh, frozen, or powdered (Asian grocery stores always carry it in at least one form), but if you can't find any, substitute 1 or 2 cloves of minced garlic. The flavor will be less Thai influenced but still delicious.

To mince lemongrass: Cut off and discard green tops down to white fleshy part. Cut off and discard root. Peel away outer layers until you reach the tender part inside. Slice very thinly across the stalk. Continue to chop with a chef's knife until very fine. **SERVES 2–3**

1–1½ tablespoons red curry paste (use the lesser amount for milder heat)

1 (15-ounce) can light coconut milk, shaken, plus more to taste

1½ tablespoons coconut oil

1 tablespoon minced fresh lemongrass (see head note) or ½ tablespoon powdered lemongrass

¾ teaspoon turmeric

1 large delicata squash (about 1¼ pounds), halved, seeded, and cut into quarter-inch half moons

¾ teaspoon kosher salt

1 (15-ounce) can chickpeas (garbanzo beans), drained and rinsed

4 ounces spinach, torn into small pieces (about 4 cups)

2 tablespoons fresh lime juice

2 cups cooked quinoa or brown rice

Mix curry paste with 1 tablespoon coconut milk and set aside. In a Dutch oven or large nonstick skillet, heat coconut oil over medium heat. Add lemongrass and cook, stirring, for 1 to 2 to minutes, until fragrant. Add curry paste mixture and turmeric to pan and cook, stirring, for a minute or so. Add squash and salt, stirring to coat. Cook for 3 to 4 minutes. Pour remaining coconut milk over the top and stir to combine. Bring to a boil, then reduce to a light simmer and cover. Cook for 20 minutes, then stir in chickpeas and spinach. Return to a simmer, cover, and cook for another 20 minutes, or until squash pierces easily with a fork. To thicken liquid, simmer uncovered for another 5 minutes. (If you like more "broth," add additional ½ cup coconut milk.) Stir in lime juice, then taste and adjust salt if needed. Serve over quinoa or brown rice. ⟡

BROWN BUTTER DELICATA DONUTS WITH SIMPLE VANILLA GLAZE

As the leaves begin to turn and the fall winds blow in, there's no reason to let pumpkin steal the show. Delicata squash is sweeter and less watery than pumpkin, yielding tender and irresistible donuts. Browned butter takes them to a whole different level, adding a heavenly, caramel depth that's difficult to duplicate. Dipped in a simple vanilla glaze, these baked donuts are even somewhat healthy, the best Sunday-morning treat a person could ask for.

You don't have to brown the butter, but the deep flavor it imparts is magical. Melt the butter in a small saucepan on the stove. Continue cooking over medium-high heat until it boils and begins to brown, stirring frequently. The butter will start to bubble and foam. Watch carefully as lightly browned specks form at the bottom of the pan. Smell the butter: it should have a nutty aroma, and a honey color. Remove from heat and pour into a separate bowl to stop the cooking. **MAKES 6–8 DONUTS**

>>

....

1 cup all-purpose flour (or 140 grams gluten-free
   all-purpose flour mix; see pages 9–10)

1 teaspoon baking powder

pinch kosher salt

½ teaspoon cinnamon

1 teaspoon pumpkin pie spice

3 tablespoons browned butter (see head note), cooled

¾ cup delicata squash puree (or another winter squash; do not
   use acorn or spaghetti; see master technique, page 75)

1 large egg, lightly beaten

½ cup packed brown sugar

1 teaspoon vanilla

GLAZE

1 cup powdered sugar

1–2 tablespoons milk

1 teaspoon vanilla

....

Preheat oven to 350 degrees (or preheat donut machine). Lightly grease a doughnut pan; set aside. In a medium mixing bowl, stir together flour, baking powder, salt, and spices. In a separate mixing bowl, whisk together browned butter, squash puree, egg, sugar, and vanilla. Carefully fold the wet mixture into the dry and stir until just combined, being careful not to over-mix.

Fill the prepared doughnut pan or machine with the batter using a small spoon or a pastry bag (a plastic bag with corner snipped off works well), filling each doughnut mold two-thirds of the way full. Bake 8 to 9 minutes in oven (or according to donut machine directions), until doughnuts are puffed and light golden brown. Remove from oven and allow doughnuts to cool for 3 minutes before turning them out onto a wire rack to fully cool.

Whisk together the powdered sugar, milk, and vanilla until smooth. The glaze will seem thick, which will help it cling to the donut. To thin, add more milk a teaspoon at a time. Dip the cooled donuts in the glaze and return to wire rack to set for about a half hour—if you can wait that long. ✧

SWEET DELICATA PIE WITH PECAN PRALINE

I'm sorry to say it, Mr. Pumpkin Pie—you've been replaced. Delicata squash is the shining star here, rich and creamy, with brown sugar notes that make merry with pecans and fall spices. You could substitute butternut squash or a sugar pumpkin, but neither offers the dense flesh or sweetness of delicata. The salty yet sweet oat crust is foolproof and naturally gluten free to boot. And the candied pecan topping? It's the deal closer that'll have your friends scraping the plate and declaring it the best pie they've ever tasted. **MAKES ONE 9-INCH PIE**

> >

Sweet Delicata Pie with Pecan Praline

....

CRUST

  1 cup plus 2 tablespoons old-fashioned oats

¾ cup oat flour (make your own: use a food processor to grind ¾ cup old-fashioned oats to a powder-like consistency)

¼ cup ground pecans

  6 tablespoons (¾ stick) unsalted butter, melted

2½ tablespoons packed dark brown sugar

  pinch kosher salt

FILLING

1¾ cup delicata squash puree (from 2 small or 1 large delicata; see master technique, page 75)

  1 teaspoon pumpkin pie spice

½ teaspoon cinnamon

½ teaspoon ground ginger

  1 teaspoon vanilla

¾ cup milk (dairy or nondairy)

¾ cup packed dark brown sugar

  2 large eggs

PRALINE

  2 tablespoons unsalted butter

  pinch sea salt

½ cup chopped pecans

  2 tablespoons dark brown sugar

  2 tablespoons pure maple syrup

  whipped cream

....

Preheat oven to 375 degrees. Grease bottom and sides of 9-inch pie pan. In a bowl, stir together all crust ingredients with a fork so everything is coated with the butter. Press firmly into pan, covering bottom and about halfway up the sides. Bake for 8 to 10 minutes. A nice, toasty fragrance signals the crust is done. Remove from oven and let cool on wire rack for 15 minutes. Reduce oven temperature to 350 degrees.

While crust is baking, add squash puree, spices, vanilla, milk, and brown sugar to bowl of food processor. Process until completely smooth. Add eggs and pulse until just incorporated, being careful not to over-mix. When crust has cooled, pour in filling and smooth top, then lightly tap on counter to let contents settle evenly.

Bake about 50 minutes, checking for doneness at 45 minutes. To avoid baking it into a soufflé that will crack, remove pie from oven when the filling is set and puffing ever so slightly, giving a little shimmy if you shake the pan lightly. The pie will firm up as it chills. Cool pie on a wire rack, then chill in the fridge for at least 3 hours. Meanwhile, make praline.

Grease a baking sheet and set aside. Set a saucepan over medium heat and add butter to melt, swirling pan to coat the bottom. Stir in salt, pecans, and brown sugar and cook for 2 to 3 minutes, until brown sugar has dissolved. Add maple syrup and cook, stirring, until bubbling and sticky. Remove from heat; spoon and spread the praline onto prepared baking sheet to cool. Break praline into pieces for garnishing the pie.

When pie has cooled, serve with whipped cream and praline. ◇

RED KURI

Also called a baby red hubbard, the red kuri is a beautiful burnt-orange heirloom Japanese variety. I stock up on these squash in late September and October because they last up to three months if stored properly and their smaller size is perfect for two people. Prized for its flavor versatility, red kuri is not overwhelmingly sweet and has a slightly nutty finish that lends itself to many different cooking applications.

IDENTIFICATION: You've probably seen a red kuri at your local farmers market, but you may have thought it was a pumpkin of some sort. It has a similar shape and piercing reddish-orange skin but with faint taupe stripes instead of ridges. Another marker is a pointed, dry stem that turns into a tiny teardrop, giving the squash an onion-like shape. Red kuri usually weigh three to five pounds.

THE INSIDE SCOOP: The flavor of red kuri squash is sweet and nutty, reminiscent of chestnuts. The flesh is dense and dry with a deep orange hue that is truly an eye-opener. It acquires a silky, velvety texture when pureed, perfect for soups and moist baked goods. Sliced or cubed, it works well in salads or stews. Although red kuri has thick skin, it softens dramatically during cooking and is edible. If you prefer it without the skin, the easiest approach is to cut the squash in half, stabilize it on its cut sides, and then shave off the skin with a sharp knife. Red kuri has a lot of seeds for its size, but I don't recommend roasting them because they are quite large and leathery. From my experience, they never achieve the same crispiness as other varieties.

ONE EASY DISH: As plain Jane as it may seem, slicing red kuri into wedges as you would a cantaloupe, tossing with sea salt and olive oil, then roasting at 400 degrees until crispy, crunchy browned edges are hugging the pan makes for one very addicting vegetable.

No-Churn Curry Kuri Ginger Ice Cream

Squash in ice cream?! You may think this recipe sounds crazy, but the sweet and savory combination is a cool, creamy winner. I literally couldn't put my spoon down after the first bite. Using sweet and lush red kuri squash, this curry concoction is truly one of a kind. The vanilla cream is the perfect counter to the warm curry spices and candied ginger, creating a harmonious bite nothing short of grown-up ice cream heaven. With only seven ingredients to this recipe, make sure they are all of the best quality. **MAKES 1 QUART**

1½ cups heavy cream, chilled

1 (14-ounce) can sweetened condensed milk

¾ cup red kuri squash puree (see master technique, page 75)

1 teaspoon sweet curry powder

½ teaspoon cinnamon

¼ teaspoon kosher salt

¼ cup finely chopped candied ginger

With a stand or hand mixer, whip the heavy cream until stiff peaks form. (Be careful not to over-mix: cream can change quickly from fluffy to butter.) Set aside. In a large mixing bowl, whisk together sweetened condensed milk, squash puree, curry powder, cinnamon, and salt. With a large spatula, gently fold in one-third of the whipped cream and all of the candied ginger. Fold in remaining cream until combined. Pour into an airtight freezer container or a loaf pan; seal or cover tightly with plastic wrap. Place in freezer and allow to harden for 4 to 5 hours before serving. ◇

AUTUMN HARVEST BREAKFAST BREAD

Dare I say this cozy quick bread might be perfection? It's moist and tender from buttery winter squash and bananas, their flavors marrying beautifully. You'll notice there isn't much added sugar in this recipe; the natural sweetness is quite enough. Since the squash and bananas are essentially "liquid" ingredients, less butter is needed to keep the bread moist, yielding an overall healthier treat. Fresh ginger and dark rum are key elements, giving the bread a signature flavor that'll have everyone asking for the recipe. The beauty of this bread is that it becomes more complex with time, staying fresh for days. Warm and toasted, it's comforting on chilly mornings or even as a late-night snack with a smear of honey. **MAKES ONE 9X5–INCH LOAF**

6 tablespoons (¾ stick) unsalted butter,
  slightly melted and whisked to a creamy texture

⅓ cup white sugar

⅓ cup packed dark brown sugar

2 large eggs

¾ cup red kuri squash puree (see master technique, page 75)

1 cup mashed, very ripe bananas (about 2–3 medium)

2 tablespoons dark rum

1 teaspoon vanilla

1½ cups plus 1 tablespoon all-purpose flour (or 210 grams
  gluten-free all-purpose flour mix; see pages 9–10)

¼ teaspoon baking powder

1 teaspoon baking soda

¼ teaspoon kosher salt

2 teaspoons cinnamon

2 teaspoons freshly grated ginger

Preheat oven to 350 degrees. Grease a 9x5–inch loaf pan. In a large bowl, whisk together the butter, sugars, eggs, squash puree, bananas, rum, and vanilla. In a separate bowl, stir together the flour, baking powder, baking soda, salt, cinnamon, and ginger. Add half of dry ingredients to wet and stir a few times. Then stir in remaining dry ingredients until just combined and no flecks of flour remain. Spoon batter into prepared pan.

Bake bread for 50 to 60 minutes, checking for doneness with a wooden pick after 40 minutes. If bread is browning but not quite finished, cover lightly with foil. When wooden pick comes out clean, remove bread from oven, let cool in pan for 8 minutes, then turn out and cool completely on a wire rack. Wrapped in aluminum foil, will last up to 4 days at room temperature. Also freezes well. ◇

CREAMY RED KURI CARBONARA WITH CHICKEN AND SPINACH

I'm going to let you in on a little secret. Pureed squash is one of my ultimate weapons in making healthy sauces with the same rich and luxurious qualities of butter and cream. The squash packs in plenty of nutrients, including fiber, potassium, magnesium, and vitamins A and C. For this "carbonara," the squash, onions, and garlic are conveniently roasted together, saving lots of prep time. This easy sauce is thickened with some of the reserved, starchy pasta water. Tossed with chicken sausage and fresh spinach, this healthy fall pasta is one you can feel good about eating. **SERVES 4**

SAUCE

- 1 small red kuri squash (about 1½ pounds), halved and seeded
- 1 small onion, halved and sliced into half moons
- 2 cloves garlic, peeled
- 1 tablespoon olive oil
- ½ teaspoon kosher salt
- ¼ teaspoon black pepper
- 2 tablespoons chopped fresh sage
- ¾ cup water
- ½ cup ricotta cheese

PASTA

- 8 ounces dried linguine (or gluten-free pasta)
- 1 pound ground chicken or chicken sausage links thinly sliced into rounds
- 2 cups chopped spinach, firmly packed
- fresh parsley for garnish
- shaved Parmesan cheese for garnish

Preheat oven to 400 degrees. Place squash cut side down on a baking sheet. Toss onions and garlic with olive oil and wrap in aluminum foil packet. Place on baking sheet with squash and roast everything for about 40 minutes, until vegetables are tender and lightly browned and squash pierces easily with a fork. Remove from oven and scoop out ¾ cup squash flesh, saving remaining flesh for another use.

Add squash puree, onions and garlic, salt, pepper, sage, water, and ricotta to blender. Blend on medium speed until smooth. Taste and adjust seasonings if needed. Set aside.

Cook linguine according to package directions. Meanwhile, if using ground chicken, cook in a skillet over medium heat, stirring in ½ teaspoon salt and breaking apart into crumbles. Cook until no longer pink, about 4 to 5 minutes. If using sausage, do not add salt; cook until heated through.

When pasta is al dente, reserve ½ cup cooking water, then drain pasta but do not rinse. Return pasta to pot, then stir in spinach and chicken. Pour sauce over top and use tongs to mix, stirring in reserved water as needed to achieve preferred creaminess. Garnish with fresh parsley and a generous amount of Parmesan. ◇

Creamy Red Kuri Carbonara with Chicken and Spinach

AFRICAN RED KURI PEANUT STEW

At first glance you may think the ingredient list for this hearty vegetarian stew is too long for your liking, but rest assured that it's every bit worth it. Made with lively African spices like ginger, fenugreek, and coriander, this healthy and satisfying meal will warm you to the core on a chilly winter evening. I like to use red kuri for its gentle sweetness, lovely chestnut flavor, and ability to stay perfectly cubed throughout the braise, but butternut would also work. The silky-smooth richness in this stew is courtesy of the peanut butter, just enough to make it luxurious without becoming cloyingly sweet. **SERVES 6**

....

- 1 small to medium red kuri squash (about 3 pounds), halved and seeded
- 1½ tablespoons olive oil
- 2 cloves garlic, minced
- 1 medium onion, finely chopped
- kosher salt
- 1 teaspoon ground ginger
- ¼ teaspoon cloves
- ¼ teaspoon ancho chile powder, plus more to taste
- 1 teaspoon ground coriander
- ½ teaspoon fenugreek seeds
- ½ teaspoon black pepper
- 2¾ cups low-sodium vegetable broth
- 1 (15-ounce) can fire-roasted crushed tomatoes
- ½ cup finely chopped red bell pepper
- ½ cup plus 1 tablespoon natural, smooth peanut butter
- 2½–3 cups thinly sliced collard greens or Swiss chard
- cooked quinoa or brown rice for serving
- cilantro for garnish (optional)

....

Place squash cut side down onto cutting board and use sharp knife or vegetable peeler to remove skin. Cut into one-inch cubes.

In a 5-quart Dutch oven or heavy-bottomed stockpot, heat oil over medium-high heat. Add garlic, onion, and big pinch of salt. Cook, stirring, for 4 to 5 minutes, until onions are soft and translucent. Stir in ginger, cloves, chile powder, coriander, fenugreek, black pepper, and 1 teaspoon salt. Cook over medium heat for about 1 to 2 minutes, stirring to create a paste. Next add in squash, broth, tomatoes, and red pepper. Bring to a boil, then reduce to a simmer and cook, covered, for about 20 minutes, stirring occasionally. Stir in peanut butter, swiss chard, and 1 teaspoon salt. (The sauce will continue to thicken as it cooks because of the starch released from the squash.) Cook at a slow simmer, lightly covered, for another 30 or so minutes, until squash is fork tender. (Be sure to test it: red kuri holds its shape so well you may think it is not done when in fact it has softened.) Taste and adjust salt and chile powder if needed. Cook uncovered an additional 5 minutes to thicken the stew if you like. Serve over quinoa or brown rice and garnish with fresh cilantro if desired. ✧

Spiced Winter Squash Cheesecake with Dark Chocolate Drizzle

I'm quite fond of one-bowl desserts like this pure and simple spiced winter squash cheesecake. It bakes and slices like a dream, and there's no crust to compete with its smooth, luscious texture. Yes, I said no crust, which also makes it naturally gluten free and a bit lighter, yet nothing short of irresistible. Let your artistic side come out when you drizzle on the dark chocolate, treating the cheesecake as your blank canvas. **MAKES ONE 10-INCH CHEESECAKE**

- 2 (8-ounce) packages cream cheese, softened
- ¼ cup sour cream
- 2 tablespoons cornstarch
- 2 large eggs, at room temperature
- 1 cup red kuri squash puree (or acorn or butternut; see master technique, page 75)
- 1 cup sugar
- 1¼ teaspoons cinnamon
- pinch cloves
- 1 teaspoon freshly grated ginger
- 1 teaspoon vanilla
- 2 ounces high-quality, 75 percent dark chocolate

Preheat oven to 350 degrees. Coat a 10-inch springform pan with non-stick spray. Using an electric mixer, beat cream cheese, sour cream, and cornstarch until smooth. Add eggs, squash puree, sugar, cinnamon, cloves, ginger, and vanilla. Mix until smooth. Pour batter into prepared pan. Bake for about 35 minutes or until cheesecake is just set. (Gently shake the cheesecake: if only a small circle in the center jiggles slightly, it is done.) Remove from oven and let cool in pan on a wire rack. Cover and refrigerate overnight to allow flavors to bloom.

The next day, carefully run a knife around the outer edges of cheesecake and release lock from pan. If moisture appears, pat the top dry with a paper towel. Finely chop the chocolate and place it in a heatproof bowl over a pan of simmering water. Stir until just melted. Drizzle chocolate onto cheesecake in whatever pattern you like and let set for 30 minutes. Will keep in refrigerator for 4 days. Also freezes well. ◇

BLUE HUBBARD

It may be big, bad, blue, and warty, but lo and behold, this ugly behemoth of the squash world shows that beauty really can be made from the beast. You'll find blue hubbards sitting alone at the farmers market, ignored by most shoppers, but the smart and curious know that this squash has some of the best flesh of all. Their thick covering allows them to be stored for the longest of any winter squash, a blessing when February rolls around and fresh produce is hard to come by in the Midwest.

IDENTIFICATION: Tipping the scales at anywhere from five to thirty pounds, this teardrop-shaped squash can come in a variety of colors, most often a bluish gray. With skin covered in warts and nodules, hubbards surely aren't the prom queen of winter squash. Luckily, given its cumbersome size, growers and grocery stores are now selling precut slices. If you do buy one whole, you'll find the sweet side of this Jekyll and Hyde vegetable once you pierce through the bumpy skin, which has a tendency to splinter off in pieces. The dense, yellow flesh is surprisingly moist, even after long storage. After the last of the blue-gray hide is peeled off, it's ready for a fairy tale transformation.

THE INSIDE SCOOP: While it is possible to cook a hubbard squash whole, its sheer bulk makes doing so an inconvenience. What I've found works best is to crack it open with a hammer or loosely wrap it in a garbage bag, hold it above your head, and drop it on the cement. No joke. It's actually kind of liberating. From there, cut the squash into manageable pieces and bake for about fifteen to twenty minutes at 300 degrees. After prebaking, scrape away the seeds, peel, and cut into cubes. You'll find that the preliminary cooking makes it much easier to work with, after which the flesh is ready to be steamed, roasted, or sautéed. The bright interior is sweet (especially if it has been stored for several months) and dry after being cooked, making a rather thick and starchy puree, ideal for gorgeous soups, stews, or pies.

ONE EASY DISH: To make a coconut-ginger-squash soup, break off a large chunk of squash and rub the skin and flesh with coconut oil. Sprinkle with salt, then roast at 400 degrees for 40 to 45 minutes, until flesh pierces easily with a fork. Scoop flesh away from skin and transfer to a blender. Add 1 can coconut milk, 1 tablespoon minced fresh ginger, and 2 tablespoons minced cilantro. Blend on high, adding water as needed to create the thickness you desire. Taste and adjust salt if needed. Garnish with chopped peanuts and additional cilantro.

THREE SISTERS CHEESY SALSA VERDE DIP

This warm, spicy dip is an ode to the Native American practice of planting beans, corn, and squash together because each "sister" was instrumental in the success of the others' growth. The corn's tall stalks were perfect for the bean's climbing vines, and the bean's roots captured nitrogen from the air to enrich the soil while the squash's large leaves shaded the shallow roots. Pure agricultural brilliance. Serve this appetizer with tortilla chips and a salty margarita for the ultimate party pleaser. **SERVES 8–10 AS AN APPETIZER**

1 (8-ounce) package cream cheese, softened

¼ cup light sour cream

¾ cup salsa verde (tomatillo salsa)

¼ teaspoon red pepper flakes, plus more for garnish

kosher salt

1½ cups colby jack or mozzarella cheese, divided

¾ cup blue hubbard (or butternut or buttercup) squash puree (see master technique, page 75)

¾ cup sweet corn (fresh or frozen)

1 (15-ounce) can pinto beans, drained and rinsed

1 clove garlic, minced

1 teaspoon cumin

¼ teaspoon cayenne

fresh chives for garnish

tortilla chips for serving

Preheat oven to 350 degrees. Coat bottom and sides of a 9-inch glass pie pan with nonstick spray. In a bowl, mix together cream cheese, sour cream, salsa verde, red pepper flakes, and ¼ teaspoon salt until smooth. In a separate bowl, combine 1 cup cheese, ¼ teaspoon salt, and the remaining ingredients except chives and chips.

Spread half of cream cheese mixture evenly across bottom of prepared pan. Top with vegetable and cheese mixture, spreading evenly with your hands to cover cream cheese layer. Spread remaining cream cheese mixture across the vegetable layer and top with remaining ½ cup of cheese. Bake for 25 minutes, checking after 15 minutes. If top layer is browning quickly, cover loosely with foil. Dish is finished when cheese is bubbling. Remove from oven, then garnish with chives and crushed red pepper flakes. Serve hot with tortilla chips. ◊

Autumn Risotto with Roasted Squash and Crispy Bacon

Risotto is one of my favorite dishes because it moves gracefully with the seasons, like this forkful of autumn, with nutty squash, delicate leeks, and fresh thyme. Envision yourself hosting a dinner party: stirring the rice, mixing a cocktail, stirring the rice, nibbling on an appetizer, all while chatting with friends! The sweet, chestnut-flavored pillows of hubbard squash fold beautifully into the creamy risotto and are supported by the salty bacon and Parmesan. A splash of balsamic vinegar may seem like an afterthought, but its acid is key to enlivening the flavors. This risotto is the precise definition of comfort food, capturing the essence of fall in the most delicious way.

Timesaver tip: The squash and bacon can be prepared up to two days ahead; the rest of the method is quite simple. **SERVES 4–5**

....

SQUASH

3 cups peeled, seeded blue hubbard (or butternut) squash, cut into quarter-inch cubes

2 tablespoons olive oil

1 tablespoon pure maple syrup

½ teaspoon kosher salt

pinch black pepper

RISOTTO

2 tablespoons olive oil

1 cup thinly sliced leeks, white and light green parts

2 cloves garlic, minced

1½ cups Arborio rice

¾ cup dry white wine

5–6 cups low-sodium vegetable stock, warmed

2 sprigs thyme

½ teaspoon kosher salt

½ teaspoon black pepper

⅛ teaspoon cinnamon

1½ tablespoons butter

½ cup grated Parmesan cheese, divided

2 tablespoons minced fresh sage

4–5 slices bacon, cooked and crumbled

balsamic vinegar

....

Preheat oven to 400 degrees. Toss squash with oil, maple syrup, salt, and pepper, then spread onto baking sheet. Roast for 30 to 35 minutes, until squash pierces easily with a fork but still holds together. Remove from oven and set aside.

In a large skillet, heat olive oil over medium heat. Add in leeks and garlic and cook, stirring, for about 5 minutes, until softened. Stir in rice, coating with oil and vegetable mixture. Cook, stirring, about 2 minutes, until rice is translucent with a white spot in the middle, looking somewhat like a tooth, then stir in wine. Cook, stirring constantly, until wine has been absorbed. Add a few ladles of broth, just enough to barely cover rice, as well as thyme, salt, pepper, and cinnamon. Cook over medium heat until broth has been absorbed, stirring constantly. Continue cooking and stirring rice, adding a cup of broth at a time, until all is absorbed and rice is tender but still firm to the bite, about 18 to 20 minutes. Turn off heat, remove thyme sprigs, and stir in butter, squash, ⅓ cup of Parmesan, and sage. Taste and adjust seasonings.

The rice should be creamy, with a little liquid left in the dish so that when you put it in a bowl it will spread a bit, indicating it hasn't been overcooked. To serve, put the risotto into individual bowls, then top each with remaining Parmesan, crumbled bacon, and a drizzle of balsamic vinegar.

Leftovers idea: Form the leftover risotto into quarter-inch-thick patties, dip in a beaten egg, then lightly dust with flour. Heat 3 tablespoons oil in a nonstick skillet over moderately high heat until hot, then cook patties, turning once, until browned. ◇

SALTED CARAMEL CHOCOLATE CHUNK BLONDIE BARS

This cookbook wouldn't be complete without a midwestern classic: dessert "bars"—sweet treats made with pantry staples and layered in a pan to resemble brownies, cookies, or pie. You'll find these concoctions cut neatly and served at church potlucks or family gatherings, every gal usually having her own "special recipe." My mom's was a chocolate chip blondie, similar to a flat and chewy chocolate chip cookie, but her secret was a sprinkling of sea salt to create that irresistible salty-sweet combination. Using her bars as inspiration, I created my own "special recipe." Loaded with chocolate chunks, boasting a gooey layer of salted caramel, and wonderfully moist from pureed winter squash, these tasty squares will be requested time after time.

MAKES ONE 9X9–INCH PAN

- 6 tablespoons (¾ stick) unsalted butter, softened
- ¾ cup lightly packed brown sugar
- ¾ cup winter squash puree (blue hubbard or kabocha; see master technique, page 75)
- 1 large egg, at room temperature
- 1 teaspoon vanilla
- 1 cup plus 2 tablespoons all-purpose flour (or 155 grams all-purpose gluten-free flour mix; see pages 9–10)
- ½ teaspoon baking soda
- pinch cinnamon
- pinch kosher salt
- 1¼ cups dark chocolate chunks
- 15 vanilla caramels
- 2 tablespoons heavy cream
- coarse sea salt

Preheat oven to 350 degrees. Coat a 9x9–inch pan with nonstick spray. Using a stand or hand mixer, beat butter and brown sugar for 1½ to 2 minutes. Mixture should be fluffy and creamy. Add in squash, egg, and vanilla, beating on low speed for 15 seconds to combine. In a separate bowl, mix together flour, baking soda, cinnamon, and salt. Add to wet ingredients, and mix on low speed until combined and smooth. Stir chocolate into dough and then, using a spatula coated with nonstick spray, press half of dough evenly into prepared pan.

Place caramels and heavy cream in a heatproof bowl. Microwave caramels on high until melted, stirring every 20 seconds. This step will take about 2 minutes, depending on your microwave. Drizzle hot caramel over dough in pan. Sprinkle with sea salt. Drop spoonfuls of remaining batter over the caramel and spread dough until caramel is mostly covered. Sprinkle bars with additional sea salt.

Bake for 20 to 25 minutes or until the top of the bars is light golden brown and the edges start to pull away from the pan. Cool on a wire rack to room temperature. Cut bars into squares and serve. ◇

SILKY BLUE HUBBARD PUDDING WITH TOASTED MACADAMIA NUTS

My first spoonful of roasted blue hubbard squash, so sweet and velvety, was a "you had me at hello" moment. This creamy stovetop pudding was inspired by fellow cookbook author and blogger Shanna Mallon. The smooth, warm custard comes together in less than fifteen minutes, and the simplicity makes it one of my most relied-upon desserts. I like to top mine with toasted macadamia nuts and crushed graham crackers, but boozy whipped cream wouldn't hurt either. You can substitute canned pumpkin or even butternut squash, but the result won't be quite as sweet, so adjust maple syrup accordingly. SERVES 5

....

¾ cup blue hubbard squash puree (see master technique, page 75)

1 cup 2 percent milk

¼ cup heavy cream

⅓ cup pure maple syrup

2 tablespoons cornstarch

pinch kosher salt

2 large eggs

1 teaspoon vanilla

¼ teaspoon cinnamon

toasted macadamia nuts

crushed graham crackers

whipped cream

....

Place squash puree, milk, cream, maple syrup, cornstarch, salt, and eggs in a blender and blend on medium until combined. Pour into a saucepan and set over medium-low heat, stirring constantly. Don't allow mixture to come to a boil (the eggs will curdle); warm it enough to create steam and a few bubbles around the edges. Continue stirring for about 8 to 10 minutes. It will look thick and spoonable, just like traditional stovetop pudding, and it should coat the back of your spoon. Remove from heat and stir in vanilla and cinnamon.

Pour into small dishes and top with macadamia nuts and graham crackers or whipped cream. Refrigerate leftovers with plastic wrap coating the surface (to avoid a gooey film) for up to 3 days. ◇

KABOCHA

The kabocha, a native Japanese squash (also referred to as a hokkaido), is a favorite in Asian cooking but also one that stole my heart with its honeylike sweetness. It matures and ripens off the vine, and as the starches convert to sugar, the flesh transforms into a prized dry, fine-grained meat. Interestingly enough, kabocha continues to grow even after it is harvested, reaching peak ripeness about two months later. Stored properly, these squash will last for up to five months, perfect for use throughout the lengthy midwestern winter. The buttercup, developed in 1932 at North Dakota Agricultural College, is what I think of as the American version of kabocha, both in size and in its super-sweet, dry meat. It was developed as "a sweet potato substitute for a northern housewife, something that could be cut and peeled easily and so good there would be no leftovers." You will see it at many midwestern markets, and the buttercup and kabocha can be used interchangeably in cooking.

IDENTIFICATION: The kabocha has a somewhat warty, dark-green or orange rind and a round shape with a flat bottom resembling a loaf of French boule. Fully ripened, the succulent kabocha will have a hard skin with a dry, corky stem and blazing reddish-orange flesh, a color recognized by many midwesterners as "hunter orange." If the stem is green at all, the squash is not quite ripe. Although the skin looks tough and irregular, it softens when cooked and becomes perfectly edible. A buttercup is also round and dark green, but a little smaller and chunkier, with a distinctive bubble-like knob on the blossom end. If you're cooking for two and don't want leftovers, the buttercup will be a more economical choice.

THE INSIDE SCOOP: The very sweet, starchy flesh of these two squash makes for amazing desserts and creamy soups. Kabocha squash also absorbs flavors beautifully; when added to salads, it soaks up the dressing for maximum flavor. While the skin on a kabocha is thick, it's not particularly hard. If you need to dice the squash, cut off a big slice, then cut that slice into manageable pieces to be roasted or steamed. Roasting results in a rich, autumnal flavor with a dense, flaky texture, while steaming yields velvety, fresh-tasting flesh. The first time you make kabocha, brush a cooked wedge with just a slick of butter to taste its pure decadence. You will be amazed.

ONE EASY DISH: In a blender combine ½ cup roasted kabocha squash puree, ½ cup yogurt, ½ cup milk, 3 ice cubes, 2 tablespoons honey, ½ teaspoon cinnamon, and freshly grated nutmeg. Blend on high for 30 seconds and enjoy a healthy smoothie.

Kabocha "Frites" with Spicy Sriracha Dip

Although these "frites" aren't quite the ones I'm in love with at my favorite French restaurant, they are quite addicting in their own right—starchy, sweet, and slightly crunchy. I got in the habit of roasting wedges of kabocha squash for use throughout the week but found myself nibbling on them throughout the day, each bite bringing me back for more. Then I decided to try them crusted in breadcrumbs, lemon zest, and parsley. Whoa. I bet you can't eat just one! **SERVES 3–4**

....

½ cup sour cream

1½ teaspoons fresh lime juice

2 teaspoons sriracha, or to taste

olive oil

½ cup breadcrumbs

1½ tablespoons minced fresh parsley

kosher salt

zest of 1 lemon

1 small kabocha squash (about 1½ pounds)

....

Mix together sour cream, lime juice, and sriracha. Set aside. (You could also use ½ cup ketchup with 2 teaspoons sriracha stirred in to make it dairy free.)

Preheat oven to 400 degrees and grease two baking sheets with olive oil. Mix together breadcrumbs, parsley, a pinch of salt, and lemon zest, using hands to rub in the lemon zest and infuse the mixture. Set aside. Carefully cut off the stem and any hard growths on the outside of the squash. Halve and seed squash, then slice into half-inch wedges.

In a large bowl, toss the wedges with a liberal amount of olive oil and ½ teaspoon salt. Be sure that every surface, including rind, is covered. Spread onto prepared baking sheets and roast for about 20 minutes or until wedges pierce easily with a fork. Remove from oven and sprinkle the tops of wedges with breadcrumb mixture, pressing with fingers to adhere. Set oven to broil and return wedges to oven for about 3 to 4 minutes, until lightly browned and crispy. Serve hot with dipping sauce. ◇

Kabocha "Frites" with Spicy Sriracha Dip

SMOKY KABOCHA AND ROASTED RED PEPPER SOUP

Yearning for a warming soup during the frigid Minnesota winter, I lit my inner fire with this one, deeply flavored with chiles en adobo (also labeled "chipotle peppers in adobo sauce") and roasted red peppers. Marinated in a tangy red sauce, chiles en adobo are the smoked and dried version of jalapeño peppers, bringing enough heat to make your toes tingle. Roasted kabocha squash flesh is so dense and creamy on its own, there really is no need for cream, plus it balances the heat nicely. A wonderful soup to make ahead of time and reheat right before serving, this one is an excellent choice for a dinner party starter. Also, remember that you can adjust the thickness by adding more or less stock. SERVES 4

1 small kabocha squash (about 1½ pounds), halved and seeded

olive oil

5 unpeeled cloves garlic

¾ cup chopped onion

¼ teaspoon celery seed

1 (24-ounce) jar roasted red peppers, drained and coarsely chopped

1½ tablespoons minced chiles en adobo (found in the Mexican food section or by the hot sauce)

½ teaspoon dried oregano

1½ teaspoons kosher salt

2¾ cups low-sodium vegetable broth, plus more as needed

2½ teaspoons apple cider vinegar

¼ cup half-and-half (optional)

toasted bread or tortilla chips for serving

Preheat oven to 400 degrees. Place squash cut side down on baking sheet. Rub a little olive oil onto unpeeled garlic cloves and wrap in aluminum foil packet. Set on baking sheet with squash and place in oven, roasting for about 45 minutes, until the flesh is tender all the way through to the skin. The outer skin will be slightly blistered and browned; the inner flesh soft and caramelized around the edges. Remove squash and garlic from oven and let cool. Scoop out flesh from squash and squeeze garlic from skins. Set aside.

While squash is roasting, heat 1½ tablespoons olive oil over medium heat in a stockpot or Dutch oven. Add onion and celery seed, stirring to coat, and cook for 7 to 8 minutes, until onion is translucent and soft. Add roasted red peppers to pot along with minced chiles, oregano, and salt. Cook, stirring, for 2 minutes, then add broth and simmer for 5 minutes.

Add squash flesh, garlic cloves, and vinegar to pot. Next, puree soup to desired consistency with either an immersion blender or, working in batches, a blender. Taste and adjust salt as needed; add broth if soup is too thick. Stir in half-and-half if desired. Serve with warm toasted bread or crunchy tortilla chips. ◇

Roasted Winter Vegetables with Lentils and Creamy Horseradish Dressing (page 154)

ROASTED WINTER VEGETABLES WITH LENTILS AND CREAMY HORSERADISH DRESSING

Many winter vegetables hide behind a tough, thick exterior, but the transformation that occurs when they are roasted or braised is a thing of beauty. Horseradish and parsley were meant to be accompaniments to vegetables, especially the sweet and slightly nutty kabocha squash. Its brilliant, blaze-orange flesh and edible skin make it one of the easiest squash to work with, like delicata. Layered on a bed of peppery lentils, the earthy tones of the winter roots get a wake-up call from a kicky horseradish sauce and brightening lemon zest. If you have a different vegetable like cauliflower or rutabaga on hand, make substitutions as you like. Feel free to prepare the lentils and dressing a day ahead. **SERVES 6 AS A SIDE DISH**

DRESSING

½ cup buttermilk

¼ cup mayonnaise

1½ tablespoons prepared horseradish, or to taste

¼ teaspoon black pepper

¼–½ teaspoon kosher salt, to taste

1 tablespoon minced fresh chives

1 tablespoon minced fresh parsley

VEGETABLES AND LENTILS

1 pound parsnips, peeled, quartered lengthwise, and cut into one-inch pieces

1 pound rainbow carrots, peeled, quartered lengthwise, and cut into one-inch pieces

3 tablespoons olive oil, divided

kosher salt

black pepper

1 pound kabocha squash, seeded and cut into quarter-
 to half-inch cubes (or use peeled, seeded butternut)

2 cups water

1 cup dried French green lentils

1 clove garlic, minced

1 tablespoon minced fresh parsley, plus more for garnish

zest of 1 lemon

minced fresh chives for garnish

....

Whisk together dressing ingredients, taste and adjust salt and horserad-ish, then set aside.

Preheat oven to 400 degrees. Toss parsnips and carrots with 2 tablespoons olive oil, ½ teaspoon salt, and pinch of pepper. Spread evenly on baking sheet so that pieces are not touching. Toss squash with remaining 1 table-spoon olive oil, ½ teaspoon salt, and pinch of pepper, then spread evenly on another baking sheet. Roast both pans for 35 to 40 minutes, stirring once, until all vegetables are tender and browning. Remove from oven.

While vegetables are roasting, bring water to a boil in a large saucepan. Add lentils and garlic, then reduce heat to a low simmer and cook, uncov-ered, for about 30 minutes. Add water as needed to keep the lentils barely covered. Test lentils; they are done when tender and no longer crunchy. Drain lentils and garlic, then stir in salt to taste and parsley.

To serve, spread lentils on a platter, then top with roasted vegetables. Drizzle dressing over the mixture and top with lemon zest and additional parsley and chives. Will keep in refrigerator for 4 days. ◇

CRANBERRY BUTTERCUP CLAUFOUTIS

One of the benefits of using squash puree in desserts is that its rich, creamy texture can be a replacement for fat or cream, similar to how applesauce works in baked goods. Squash's natural sweetness can also replace part of the sugar you would normally need. With both these qualities in mind, I created this seasonal claufoutis, a fancy-sounding French dessert that is quite simple to make. Buttercup squash puree is blended like a pancake batter, then studded with tart cranberries and baked into fluffy, custardy decadence. This golden cloud's texture is similar to flan, but not as heavy. I like to add fresh herbs to desserts—in this case, thyme—to give them a defining finish. SERVES 5–6

....

1	tablespoon butter
1½	cups fresh cranberries
⅓	cup plus 2 tablespoons sugar
3	large eggs
1	cup plus 2 tablespoons milk (dairy or nondairy)
½	cup buttercup (or kabocha) squash puree (see master technique, page 75)
½	cup all-purpose flour (or 70 grams all-purpose gluten-free flour mix; see pages 9–10)
1	teaspoon cinnamon
2	teaspoons minced fresh thyme
¼	teaspoon kosher salt
	powdered sugar or whipped cream for garnish

....

Preheat oven to 375 degrees. Place butter in a 9- or 10-inch glass or ceramic pie pan. Set in oven for a few minutes to melt butter. Remove pan from oven and swirl to coat bottom and sides with melted butter. Spread cranberries evenly in pan and sprinkle with 2 tablespoons sugar, then roll cranberries around to lightly coat. Set aside.

Add eggs, milk, and squash puree to a blender. Blend on low for 30 seconds to combine. Add in flour, remaining ⅓ cup sugar, cinnamon, thyme, and salt. Blend on medium for 30 seconds to mix thoroughly. Pour over cranberries. Bake for 35 to 40 minutes, until puffy and golden brown around the sides. Let pan cool for 15 minutes on a wire rack. Best served warm or at room temperature, sprinkled with powdered sugar or topped with whipped cream. ◇

Cranberry Buttercup Claufoutis

ARMENIAN NUTMEG FRIENDSHIP CAKE

This cake was made out of love for my dear friend Kelli, who shares my passion for connections and conversation made over food. She married into a 100 percent Armenian family and never looked back, embracing tradition in all ways. I decided to put my own spin on the classic Armenian nutmeg cake for her, incorporating the sweetest of squash, the kabocha. Warm and spicy, with pleasing overtones of nutmeg and walnut, it's simple to make and rustic in appeal. A rather thick batter is poured over a shortbread-like base, and as they bake together the crust becomes crisp and the batter ends up like a soft coffeecake. Eat this with friends alongside a hot cup of French press and hug them good-bye with Kelli's famous words: "I hope you had a delicious time." **MAKES ONE 8- OR 9-INCH CAKE**

- 1½ cups all-purpose flour (or 210 grams all-purpose gluten-free flour mix; see pages 9–10)
- ½ cup ground walnuts, plus ⅓ cup finely chopped walnuts for topping
- ¾ cup packed brown sugar
- 2 teaspoons baking powder
- pinch kosher salt
- 9 tablespoons unsalted butter, chilled, cut into small cubes
- ¼ teaspoon cinnamon
- ¾ cup kabocha (or buttercup) squash puree (see master technique, page 75)
- ¼ cup milk
- 1 large egg
- 2 teaspoons freshly grated nutmeg (or 1 teaspoon ground nutmeg)

Preheat oven to 350 degrees. Grease bottom and sides of a 9-inch spring-form or standard cake pan. In a large bowl, stir together flour, ½ cup ground walnuts, brown sugar, baking powder, and salt. With a pastry blender or fork, cut in butter until mixture resembles coarse breadcrumbs. Take out a third of the mixture (about a heaping cup) and add the cinnamon to it. Press this portion of the mixture firmly into the base of the prepared pan.

In a separate bowl, whisk together squash puree, milk, egg, and nutmeg until combined. Fold wet ingredients into remaining flour mixture, mixing thoroughly so no flour specks remain. Batter will be very thick. Spread over crust base. Sprinkle ⅓ cup chopped walnuts over top and bake 45 to 50 minutes or until a wooden pick inserted in the center comes out clean and edges start to brown. If cake is browning too quickly, cover lightly with foil. Allow cake to cool at least 30 minutes before removing from pan. ◇

Resources

Deborah Madison. *Vegetable Literacy: Cooking and Gardening with Twelve Families from the Edible Plant Kingdom.* Ten Speed Press, 2013.

Shanna and Tim Mallon. *Food Loves Writing.* foodloveswriting.com.

Russ Parsons. *How to Pick a Peach: The Search for Flavor From Farm to Table.* Mariner Books, 2008.

Deb Perelman. *The Smitten Kitchen.* smittenkitchen.com.

Elizabeth Schneider. *Vegetables from Amaranth to Zucchini: The Essential Reference: 500 Recipes, 275 Photographs.* William Morrow Cookbooks, 2001.

Bonny Wolf. "Winter Squash: New Faces in the Pumpkin Patch." Kitchen Window. October 27, 2010. National Public Radio. Available: www.npr.org/templates/story/story.php?storyId=130833903.

INDEX